Vikramaditya
An Archetypal Portrait

Shreeja Tripathi Sharma

ATLANTIC
PUBLISHERS & DISTRIBUTORS (P) LTD

Published by

ATLANTIC

PUBLISHERS & DISTRIBUTORS (P) LTD

7/22, Ansari Road, Darya Ganj, New Delhi-110002
Phones : +91-11-40775252, 40775214, 23273880, 23275880
Fax : +91-11-23285873
Web : www.atlanticbooks.com
E-mail : orders@atlanticbooks.com

Printed & bound in India by Atlantic Print Services

My obeisance to the lord of Time
Jai Mahakala

For the countless unknown 'Vikrams'

Preface

The reflections of this book came upon me as I drafted the synopsis for a fellowship while travelling from Bhopal to Ujjain, the legendary capital of Vikramaditya. I found myself engaged in searching archives of the king on my frequent trips to Ujjain, the city where my husband was posted.

The fellowship was awarded and my fascination for Vikramaditya and Ujjain grew stronger. Soon, I was posted as an Assistant Professor of English at Vidisha and carried to another gripping destination of the glorious Vikramaditya empire. The recollections of Vikramaditya have overwhelmed me through my journeys of his grand narrative and find a spontaneous outpouring in this work.

The historic grand narrative of the legendary king Vikramaditya is interspersed with myths and has been scrutinised suspiciously for accuracy, historic distortions, subjectivity, and the play of personal imagination. The weighty objections against the historic existence of the king due to lack of reliable numismatic and epigraphical evidence have dominated the discourse of convention in history.

Despite this, the intense engagement of Indian culture with the ideology of Vikramaditya has sustained through generations. The archetypal power of the legendary king has become a metaphor for individuation, inspiring generations of rulers to seek the venerated title, Vikramaditya.

The historical reality and the rationalised self-identity of the mortal king has arguably been wiped away, but the immortal memory of the archetypal Hero thrives in the collective memory and has been handed down orally through folk tales, sculpture, and art.

This book seeks to construct a portrait of the legendary king based on the paradigm of archetypal literary criticism. The work scans the disregarded fabulistic elements of the discourse through an archetypal lens and attempts to impart a degree of flexibility to the rigid frame of conventional, chronological, and factualist authority. It attempts to address the problematic embedded in the narrative of myths with riddled history through its focus on the archetypal core of meaning—on that constant which does not change, even in the face of change.

The work examines the numismatic evidence of punch marked coins of Ujjain, the mythic narrative, and cultural practises of the Vikramaditya tradition through an archetypal lens and synchronically traces its interlinkages with analogous parallels in world culture. The archetype as *pramana* or evidence breeds vitality to the famished narrative nearly devoid of epigraphy and recasts the deeply rooted epitome of Indian culture in a new frame.

The work rather optimistically mimics the Jungian concept of societal individuation by integrating the absent shaping influence of the past more consciously with our present and, thus, makes the ideal historic model more relevant to our spiritually fractured contemporary society. The works disassociates from the disputed self-identity of Vikramaditya, the historic person, and shifts the discourse towards the constant reality of what it terms—the 'Vikramaditya consciousness'.

The book consists of essays which propose a tentative synoptic view of an archetypal percept of Vikramaditya. The essays provoke abstract, archetypal portraits which stimulate a perceptible rather than an empirical sketch. The book leverages on the autonomy given to the transforming paradigm of historiography to augment the conventional narrative with the often-disregarded element of myths. It innovates the structure and methodology to recreate but does not undermine the central authority of the grand narrative, which it rather seeks to strengthen and reinvigorate. It recolours to restore but takes care, not disfigure as it reshapes the traditional narratives.

The first essay problematises myth as a historic narrative and describes the inherent element of fiction in the production of historic narrative from the sources of embedded myth in ancient Indian history. It introduces the problem of exiguous attention to the legend of Vikramaditya in the area of literary historiography and briefly mentions the fundamental concepts of archetypal criticism, which are discussed later in detail.

The second essay revaluates the grand narrative of the legendary king Vikramaditya with respect to the chronological records of historic and mythic context and adds an archetypal perspective to the discourse. The essay also discusses the orality of the Vikramaditya tradition and its archetypal manifestations.

The third essay provides a typological introduction to the archetypal thought, particularly with reference to its genesis and influence on literature. The essay also explores the influence of Indian thought on the archetypal theory and seeks to establish its affinity with ancient Indian historic narrative and its mythic dimensions.

The fourth essay describes Vikramaditya as an archetypal hero through a structural narrative analysis of *Vetaal Panchavimshati* within the schematic elements of the Monomyth and explores the riddled narrative of the text for archetypal elements. It draws analogies between the grand narratives of Vikramaditya and Arthur's knight Perceval to serve as specimens of the shared narrative structures exemplifying the "mystical religious quest" of the eternal spiritual problem of Mankind.

The fifth essay examines the symbolic vocabulary of numismatic art through archetypal linkages of the punch-marked coins of Ujjain, belonging to the first century BCE, available at Ashwini Research Institute, Ujjain. It explores the Jungian concept of anima through the living tradition of cultural and religious practises as exemplified in selected temples of Ujjain.

I am grateful to Vikramaditya Shoodhpeeth, Ujjain, for the award of Maharaja Vikramaditya, Junior Research Fellowship, which has made me a diminutive of a great tradition. I am extremely grateful to Dr. R.C. Thakur, President of Ashwini Research Institute, Mahidpur, for a warm and generous access to his antique and rare collection of coins. I am thankful to the office Staff of Vikramaditya Shodhpeeth, Ujjain, and Triveni

Interpretation Centre, Ujjain, for their earnest assistance in making books and manuscripts available for the research and for providing a conducive and cooperative work environment.

I am beholden to the memory of my great-grandfather, Dr. Ram Shankar Tripathi, Professor of History at Banaras Hindu University and the author of *History of Ancient India*, 1942. The prolific collection of books in his enduring library have remained a source of my constant allure and curious nourishment.

I owe everything to my family, thank-you for unconditional love, support, suggestions, and generous proof-readings.

I seek apology for any historic incongruity which may arise in the work through its adaptation in archetypal literary historiography. Though with a different approach, the book earnestly echoes the glorious historic consciousness of the Vikramaditya ideology, ethics, philosophy, culture, and world view, and seeks its reiteration within the people of India and the world. Though it speaks of literary history, it points towards a deeper revival and renewal of the spirit of Vikramaditya borne in the collective conscious of our Self.

Shreeja Tripathi Sharma

Contents

List of Pictures

CHAPTER 1
Myths in Time

1.1 Problematising the Myth of Vikramaditya as a Narrative of Literary History

The conventional approach to history construed it as an objective discipline. The construction of historical narratives involved an empirical problematisation of the past. The conventional factualist approach to history banished significant chunks of ancient Indian history on account of their interlinkages with myths. The mythic narrative of Vikramaditya was rejected by Indologists and historians despite a deeply rooted presence in the Indian culture. The historical persona of the legendary king as well as the era—*Vikram Samvat* started by him was scrutinised and excluded from the historic discourse due to unvalidated historic evidence.

The legacy of Vikramaditya, however survives in folk tradition, culture, oral, and written literature. Could such a vast tradition emerge from a void? The stiff historic structure of the narrative in this regard inevitably appeals for a more accommodating attitude particularly with regard to the post-modern approach to historiography.

The historiography has undergone a radical transformation which advocates the use of innovative techniques and practices which acknowledge the innate fictionality of historical narratives and allow greater autonomy to the reader in contrast to the factualist objectivity and the conventional centre of authority of the traditional narratives. The approach advocates the use of new methods of historiography, epistemology, and narratology.

The contemporary narratives construct meaning of the past by synchronically relating it to the present and at the same time study diachronic linkages between historic periods.

The significant departure from traditional modes of narration and the tendency to use of new approaches towards the representation of reality inseparably involve a cross examination of the earlier 'records of reality'.

Several narratives of Indian history have been disregarded due to their close allegiance with myths. The cyclical view of ancient Indian history, instead of a linear one and the inclusion of myths in the discourse of ancient history have understandably led to the expulsion of these narratives from the mainstream discourse. The popularly endorsed view recommends that the cohesion of myths in history merely reflects an infantile development of the juvenile human mind. However, it also casts the curious question: *Can distorted history become a myth? Can history reshaped into a didactic sermon turn in time into a myth?*

History and myth have always remained antithetical modes of narrative construction. The conventional approach to history construed it as an objective, empirical discipline, and emphasised a linear orientation and chronological narration. The historical representation of the past was traditionally considered an authentic representation. However, the post-modern historians have increasingly challenged the conventional façade of history.

In this transforming context of developments, the discourse is inevitably interrogated with the following questions:

1. Can the narrative now acknowledge the myths in discourse of ancient history?
2. Can the discourse now accommodate the fictional truth of literary history?

The archetypal view of the myth as an expression of the collective unconscious pivots its place in the historic discourse. The myth has served as metaphorical narrative to explain the nature of spiritual reality to man. However, they seem to belong to a domain outside the ambit of objective rationality since the earliest of scholarly deliberations.

The treatment of myth was a much-debated topic among the Greek philosophers. Plato explicitly disregarded the mythic narrative in his seminal work *Republic* as he considered it to be an expression removed from reality. However, Aristotle challenged the views of his mentor in his celebrated work *Poetics* and named the plot 'mythos' and expressed a more sympathetic treatment of the myth. The mythical conception of history has been severely assaulted by the Platonic successors. The conception of myths as the antithesis of rationality, objectivity is a transforming concept. The 'one-sided' reality has been understandably dismissing myths from the discourse of history, yet they have often built their own rooms in the evolving space of narratives.

The 18th-century Italian philosopher and historian Giambattista Vico challenged the way myths were construed by amalgamating them with their historical contexts. He advanced the view which regarded myth as the foreground to history, and he proclaimed in his famed assertion—"mythos precedes and informs logos." He was supportive of the view of history, based on the ideas of cyclical time and the role of providence, a prominent characteristic of ancient Indian history.

In India, Jyotiba Phule was among the earliest thinkers to contextualise regional history with local myths. Phule began historicising ancient myths and legends so as to preserve their ephemeral essence, but ended up constructing fictional retelling of the myths.

He historicised myths and 'unmasked' them as contemporary social constructs particularly in relation to the power equations in society.

The problematisation of myth as a narrative of ancient Indian history presents interesting peculiarities in terms of searching factual information for narrative production. For instance, if we look at the names of few ancient cities appearing in myths, some are still identifiable such as Ujjain (Ujjayani) and Bhopal (Bhojpal) in central India or some have taken new names but are still traceable for instance Vidisha (Besnagar), Mandsaur (Dashpura) or Ratlam (Ratanpuri). However, we often come across some mythic locations such as Ayodhya and Dwarka where history, archaeology, and metaphorical allegory join hands to conceal the truth.

The mythic homes of Hindu gods such as Kailash, the abode of Shiva and Vaikunth, the divine residence of Vishnu seem to be as mythic or metaphoric spaces rather than actual physical places which resonate with the promise of salvation to devotees. They reflect symbolic connotations like after-life destinations of the virtuous, rather than testifying actual earthen realities. However, the actual physical existence of the stated cannot be fairly ruled out and at the same time cannot be verified either. The integration of the so-called sacred narratives in our profane time becomes is an impossible task for building our narratives.

Due to their allegiance to imagination, myths connect more closely with fiction. They are however not just disjoint apparatus, as they may seem. Myths do possess an interesting attribute: they seem to have inherited a universally shared, common, central structure. Campbell called it the monomyth and after years of dedicated study of the myths concluded that they tend to conform to common structure.

In this context, this book explores the mythic narrative of the legendary king Vikramaditya and attempts an archetypal portrait of the king. The methodology explores the myths, which have often been confined to the genre of 'folk-tales' and 'stories for kids' and seeks to augment the discourse by recognising with due respect, what has often been largely ignored.

The dominion of myth in the fabulistic-historic narrative has been a rather ostracised convention. The narrative production of post-modern history lies near ever-blurring boundaries with fictional narratives. They are characterised by a departure from the rigid chronological structures impart flexibly and accommodate imagination and innovations. The post-modern narratives endorse fragmentary historic sketches with traces of fictionality, innovation and formation of new patterns of meta-narrative.

The narratives often challenge the conventional 'centered' discourse of the previous historical texts and are suggestive of alternative versions of conventional history. The post-modern historiography places on a continuum the contraries of— empirical and genealogical, diachronic and synchronic and so on.

The post-modern narratives also question the conventional empirical approach of history having been written from the perspective of the kings or the dominant classes and provide genealogies or alternative histories to represent the absent subaltern or marginalized classes. The diachronic emphasis of conventional narratives, based on imperial-centric power of authority like kings or dynasties lead to inevitable gaps in the narratives on account of the marginalized absence of the misrepresented or un-represented classes.

However, this book restricts its scope to the archetypal framework of literary criticism and seeks to construct the portrait of the legendary king Vikramaditya through the narrative analysis of the mythic content associated with him.

The book accommodates the transforming nature of the modern discourse, though in a limited sense. It structurally splits the narrative into essays which share overlapping boundaries between myth, literature, and history. The methodology innovatively adopts the framework of archetypal criticism for scanning the mythic content, often banished from the discourse of history.

However, the book by no means undermines the grand narrative of the most venerated legend of Indian culture. On the contrary, it adopts the archetypal approach to uphold and celebrate him as an eternal icon of inspiration. The book innovatively uses the synchronic approach to establish the legendary king as an archetypal influence across cultures. Thus, the book uses the flexibility provided by post-modern set-up to accommodate the often-ignored mythic perspectives into the discourse and seeks to echo the image of the legendary cultural hero with a more audible voice.

The task involves peculiar problems. Problematising of the myths and legends embedded in the narratives of ancient history has never been easy. Myth and history can be seen as contradictory polarities pertaining to imagination and reason. Their co-existence in ancient narratives is as difficult as it is usual and it further makes the task of an accurate production of narrative difficult because decoding and understanding what the myths are trying to say with accuracy is nearly impossible. However, the archetypal center of the myth, considered as a central core of meaning, can be seen as a recurrent constant which has not changed despite the successive transmissions and distortions through generations.

The 'historical-myth narrative' of king Vikramaditya is inextricable from his glorious myths which rekindle the collective memory of a long-lost, sacred past. Myths about him are numerous and a substantial expanse of Indian folk literature ceaselessly sparks the historic consciousness with his ephemeral memory. However, the gaps in the historic grand narrative of Vikramaditya remain unresolved due to significant factors.

First, the Vikramaditya era which begins in a temporally distant time frame, as early as the first century BCE makes the task of an accurate reconstruction nearly untenable.

Second, problematising myth in history challenges the historic perception of the king and renders the discourse of historic production unauthenticated and debilitated.

Third, the narratives of the legendary king are marked by regional and cultural variations, and contradict the details in different sources—historic accounts, myths, legends, and folk-tales, etc. Often, these narratives appear considerably anecdotal particularly due to their distortions in their oral transmission over divergent spacio-temporal recollections and the addition of the super-natural and fabulistic elements in myths.

Fourth, the historical reconstruction through content analysis, involves subjectivity, inaccuracies and inevitable play of personal imagination.

Fifth, while the faculty of Hindi literature, has a considerably significant range of works based essentially on conventional approach to historiography, we hugely lack similar research in the stream of English literary historiography and have scanty narratives which explore the transforming modes of narrative production, if at all. Moreover, Hindi literature is replete with works reminiscing the legendary king however, comparable works in the field of English literature are alarmingly few. The narrative of the great legend is said to have been first narrated in an extinct language Paishachi, from where it flowed in Sanskrit and Hindi, in several tongues and texts. It is logical that we allow the same proliferation of our cultural emblem in as many works in English literature.

Another notable point is that the works on Vikramaditya can be roughly segmented into two broad categories: (a) literary works dealing with myths and tales and (b) historical works and critical commentaries.

With respect to English literature, while we do have works belonging to the first category, i.e. myths and tales, we are lacking in works belonging to the second category particularly in keeping in mind the transformation in the art of narratology.

Sixth, conventional research treats the subject of historic reconstruction of the Vikramaditya era, diachronically and explores different kings such as Chandra Gupta II who assumed the title Vikramaditya. However, these narratives are lacking in a synchronic study of interlinkages with focus of their reflections in the present.

In this context, this book attempts a veritable portrait of the Vikramaditya based on the archetypal theory of literary criticism. The work seeks to augment and support the diachronic structure with a synchronic orientation and explores the archetypal linkages within the mythic, numismatic, and cultural components of the Vikramaditya Tradition.

A narrative on king Vikramaditya cannot escape discrepancies and subjective inaccuracies as he belongs to an era of antiquity. The archetypal approach in such a setting is useful as the narrative does not rely on details which are contradictory and scanty. It so avoids discrepancies and builds the narrative through its focus on the ephemeral essence which it seeks to capture the archetype—the unchanging constant which remains same, univocal, and analogues across variations of space, time, boundaries, borders, and cultures.

This book attempts an amalgamation of the contraries—mythic and the historic and conventional and the post-modern, through the archetypal framework to evoke a portrait of the collective unconscious, to whatever extent possible. The grand narrative of the powerful monarch proclaims his unbroken authority, yet the narrative builds his portrait highlighted by discrete archetypal parts bears the semblance of a transforming art.

The archetypal approach and structural design of the work seeks a resolution by painting a fuller life-like portrait of Vikramaditya by working on the often-neglected myths and recolours the antique portrait with fresh paints. However, as it renovates, it takes care not to disfigure the precious features of the antique art and simply adds colour, where needed to preserve and propagate the majestic art. The archetypal artist finds a middle-ground, between the graceful traditional conventions and bold post-modern redefinition. It does not build the portrait afresh or ferociously defy conventions. It transforms to preserve. It values art, whether old or new and paints to essentially tie the two!

Picture 1: Chaturbhuj Pillar, Mangalnath, Ujjain

CHAPTER 2
Remains of a Legend

2.1 Chronicles of a Legend: Vikramaditya

The relationship between the historicity and archaeology of Vikramaditya and the authenticity of his legendary story is complex, disputed, and paradoxically interrelated. The discourse of the legendary king can be grouped into two primary streams of thought. The first group of chroniclers endorse the literary and cultural tradition and consider Vikramaditya as the king of Ujjain, who reigned in the first century BCE. The second group of chroniclers disregard the mythic material as reliable historic evidence and postulate Chandra Gupta II as the representative ruler of the Vikramaditya tradition.

The historicity of the Vikramaditya era in terms of both the founder and the foundation has been a matter of historical speculation. The conjectures about the identity of Vikramaditya—the hero who expelled the foreigners, the so-called 'Sakas' from his motherland, started the epoch called '*Vikram Samvat*' and inspired a glorious age of culmination of arts, literature, and learning; remains unvalidated, vague, and shrouded in myths.

The faction which ascribes the foundation of the era *Vikram Samvat* to king Vikramaditya of 1st century BCE sharply contradicts the sceptical view which largely disregards him despite his cultural significance and the enormity of literature surrounding him; and postulates the eras—Vikrama, Malwa, and Krita as different names of the era founded in 57 BCE.

However, the conventional approach of the second group of empirical chroniclers has been has often been challenged by the first faction. Firstly, with the rationality that the inscription writers of the contemporary period were not habituated with giving proper names to the associated periods due to which the nomenclature of the historical periods may have been done much after the commencement of the actual period. Secondly, the reasoning that the nomenclature reflected the transformation of Malwa from republic to monarchy corresponds to the codification of the eras.

The legendary Vikramaditya, as per the approving classical literary chroniclers, is proposed to have been born in 101 BCE (Kali Samvat 3000) and to have become the emperor of Ujjain in 81 BCE (Kali Samvat 3020). There is a disagreement on the estimated number of years of his reign, the range of which varies significantly between 60, 86, and 100 years. It has been rather precisely described to be 135 years, 7 months, 10 days, and 15 hours in certain commentaries (Rajpurohit, *Samrat Vikramaditya aur Navratana*). Such descriptions are understandably at odds with sceptical historians due to the obvious lack of evidence in support, not to mention logical incongruities.

The 'Vikramaditya era' in a historical sense is a cultural tradition rather than a validated historical document, the enigma of which has incessantly enthralled the course of history. In contrast to the historic empirical perplexity, the literary, and mythic sources consistently portray Vikramaditya as a paragon of valour, justice, fair-play, and perfection. Indian culture revers Vikramaditya as a symbol more than a king and as a glorious tradition more than a factual physical monarch.

This book makes a departure from the conventional, disputed numerical assessment of the number of years of king Vikramaditya's reign with reference to the 'Vikramaditya Era' and rather seeks to release his influence out of the tethers of chronology into an unbound memoir of his eternal presence. The ageless archetypal portrait of the monarch as a dynamic percept rather than a static object, which flows down to us from the period of much disputed, dark antiquity. The approach disregards the controversial categorisation of the 'Vikramaditya Era' as a quantifiable numeric or epigraphic object and builds the discourse through a literary archetypal percept, emphasising the consistent flow of his 'Imago Dei-ish' reflections upon our race.

The conventional narrative of Vikramaditya with unvalidated historical proof of existence is inherently riddled with chronological ambiguity. In this context, this book seeks to build the literary narrative by mapping the archetypal portrait of the monarch through its manifestation in the archetypal patterns and through tracing its synchronic interlinkages with parallel symbols across different cultures. The art, literature, orality, and iconography which developed around the archetype of Vikramaditya is fluid and ever evolving, yet constant in its ephemeral essence, which becomes the material for the portrait of Vikramaditya.

The epigraphy of Vikramaditya, the person and the fantasy of Vikramaditya, the myth are both allusive and unvalidated. However, the authority of archetypal Vikramaditya, not the historical person, but the metaphorical benchmark of perfection is a percept which remains tenable.

The Indian tradition and culture has unanimously witnessed the veneration of 'titular Vikramadityas' across successive chronological historical periods with different Indian monarchs assuming the honorific title 'Vikramaditya' which is linked with archetypal connotations.

Vikramaditya—the 'titular symbol' much sought after by Indian monarchs who characteristically were occupied with the process of 'Becoming' perfect masters of their kingdoms, thrives as what I propose to call 'Vikramaditya archetype'. The legendary king survives in the collective memory, enduring beyond the perishable evidence of historical existence which manifests in the form of archetypal truth.

The legendary king Vikramaditya appears in literature and myths as an archetypal super hero, the epitome of justice, valour, and rightful conduct. But the question of his historicity has captured public fascination and ignited scholarly debates. The historic narrative of Vikramaditya, the real person, is ambiguous and lacking in epigraphic evidence yet Vikramaditya, the mythic hero, is evergreen and timeless.

The 'Vikramaditya archetype', is a percept, which I choose to propose as an archetypal image of Vikramaditya shared collectively and transmitted orally. It thrives as an archetypal memory and has been used in this book to build a literary profile as an alternative to the scanty records available in history which have seemingly dwindled and declined.

The Indian or specifically the Hindu tradition proclaims Vikramaditya as the universal ruler of India with his headquarters at Ujjain in Avanti or Malwa region (though, in a few early cases, he is called 'the lord of Pataliputra', the capital of Magadha). The information, however, has remained invalidated by epigraphic or historical evidence and is understandably perplexing for a historical narrative. However, the multitude myths, eulogising Vikramaditya as an ideal king, as well as his overwhelming cultural identity, have constantly challenged the objectivist nullification.

The enormity of his presence in literature naturally leads us to the question: *Could such a lavish collection of tales emerge from a void? Can the lack of historical evidence conclusively justify the narrative entirely as fiction? Does the reiteration of the hero in myths signify an obscure presence?*

Such questions have been raised by historians and have explicably remained unanswered. Vikramaditya has been best comprehended—not as a single historic person, but rather as an epitome of qualities assumed by great kings from time to time. The historical authenticity of Vikramaditya and his reign during the first century BCE is a historical puzzle. However, that several Indian kings, assumed the title Vikramaditya, is an undisputed historical fact. The truth of the king, who became an inspiration for subsequent generation of kings and who remains shrouded in myths is undeniably a mystery.

The surviving narrative of Vikramaditya projects him through images or universal attributes which exceedingly undermines the significance of tangible details. The popular legend *Simhasana Dvatrimsika*, for instance recollects the king as a paragon of thirty-two virtues praised as essential qualities of a great king. The text can be interpreted in the context of the ancient yogini-cult of spiritual practice, which was prevalent in the 7th century and unto at least the 15th century, and which arguably had been derived from a much ancient tradition.

The imagery of the king in association with his virtuous qualities is in correspondence with the Indian tradition of addressing deified beings with different names based on specific *gunas* or virtues. Likewise, the legendary king Vikramaditya has been referred by different names in myths which connote different attributes of his qualities and accomplishments. As '*Sahasanka*' or the 'one whose characteristic mark is the daring courage', he appears as an incarnation of valour and righteousness, as a redeemer of the weak and oppressed. As '*Sakari*' or 'the Enemy of the Sakas', he appears as a liberator of his motherland from foreigners, who were referred to as the Sakas. His greatest achievement apparently was the destruction of the Sakas, an event commemorated by the start of the calendar *Vikram Samvat*.

The Indian memoirs of antiquity narrate the saga of Vikramaditya in considerably many accounts. The Jain text, *Kalakacharya Kathanaka*, outlines the story about Gardabhila, the king of Ujjaiyani, who abducted Saraswati, the sister of a Jain monk named Kalaka. In order to take revenge, Kalaka approached the powerful Saka chiefs, who reigned on the territory which lied on the other side of the river Indus. The Sakas launched an attack on Gardabhila, defeated him and seized his kingdom with his capital at Ujjaiyani.

The tale remains unvalidated on account of lack of historical evidence. However, the following hypothesis logically trails from the narrative:

(a) Shortly before the Sakas invaded India, Jainism was spreading towards Ujjain and met initial resistance by the Shaivite kings of Ujjaini. There may have been ideological differences and conflicts between the Jain clerics and the king.

(b) The Jain preachers approached the Sakas, who captured Ujjaini, which was ruled by a king called Gardabhila.

To quote a translated excerpt of the account from *Vikramaditya of Ujjain* by Raj Bali Pandey:

> The Saka armies surrounded Visala (former Ujjain) like swarms of locusts and Gardabhila was captured alive but Kalaka intervened and allowed him to go into an exile in a forest. Kalaka finally recovered his sister Saraswati who lived along with a group of nuns. Kalaka was killed by a tiger while in exile in the forest. (30)

The name of the king appears as Mahendraditya in few narratives. The discrepancy in information in these narratives is apparent. However, despite the variations, most of the accounts narrate the same central story which indicates that Vikramaditya was the illustrious son of the defeated emperor Gardabhila, who sought to avenge his father. He defeated their powerful adversary the Sakas and restored his father's kingdom. This was a landmark victory and to commemorate the event, the Hindu era—the *Vikram Samvat*, was named after him. However, after about one hundred and thirty-five years after the start of the '*Vikram Samvat*', the Sakas won back Ujjayini and started the Saka era, an era of their own.

The narrative of Vikramaditya appears in several sources such as *Gathasaptashati*, a Prakrit anthology composed by Hala, the king of Pratishthana. There is yet another text, the *Brihat Katha* by Gunadhya, written in Paisachi. The original text is lost, but the tales are recounted in two important Sanskrit works, the *Brihat Kathamanjari* of Kshmendra and *Katha Saritsagar* of Somadeva.

The Jain *Pattavalis*, written in Prakrit, which record the names of rulers of Avanti chronologically, place a king named Vikramaditya about the middle of the first century BCE. The *Harivamsha* too mentions about the Gardabhila, the lineage belonging to Vikramaditya and records a list or rulers of Ujjain in chronological order.

The Puranas provide a general reference to the Gardabhilas, while the *Bhavishaya Puran* specifically mentions Vikramaditya as the king of Avanti, born to destroy the Sakas and to establish Aryan religion. The *Kumar Khand* of the *Skanda Puran* also mentions king Vikramaditya three thousand years after the beginning of the Kali Age.

Despite the reference to Vikramaditya in several texts, the evidence of his historic persona, is subject to scholarly debate on several counts. Several scholars assert that Vikramaditya belonged to the Gardabhila clan of Malwa and established the era called the *Vikram Samvat*. However, this theory is not without counter arguments as, firstly, the name Vikramaditya is not associated with the Vikrama era from the time of its foundation and has also been referred to as Krita and Malwa eras. Secondly, the post-Christian era, often refers to the Saka era rather than to *Vikram Samvat* to indicate the date of their compositions.

The purpose of this book is not a historic dissection of the rather undeterminable truth but the archetypal assimilation and synthesis of the legacy of Vikramaditya and cognizance of its shaping influence on the Indian identity, both in the past and in present.

Vikramaditya, the hero typically confirms to the archetypal structure of the 'monomyth' and is analogous to mythic parallels of several cultures. Vikramaditya as an integral element of the Indian national identity, is more of an embodiment of cultural legacy, than of history.

The legend of Vikramaditya, resides in the collective memory, living, re-emerging time and time again in popular culture, in forms such as books, comics, animation, television serials, documentaries, and visual art.

Under both conditions: that is those which look up to Vikramaditya, the historical person or those which uphold the view of the 'tradition of Vikramaditya', the quest for Vikramaditya, has been enduring. The archetypal image of Vikramaditya, is neither archaeological nor mythic. The archetypal Vikramaditya is an amalgamation of central ideas around his enduring core, which testifies that prototype paragon of Vikramaditya, who may have once lived and simultaneously sustains within, the seeds which ensure further, through collective memory, the idea that: Vikramaditya will live.

2.2 Orality and Vikramaditya Tradition

The transformation of thought from orality to writing is also the saga of evolution of mankind. However, the efficacy of oral tradition as a reliable source of historical writing has been a matter of much debate.

Oral tradition is a practice of transmission of ideas and stories through speech, which are typically handed down across generations. The oral tradition eventually transforms into a written documented text, which serves as an artefact of civilisation and culture. Texts concerning oral history are documents of preserved history. The oral history carries with it the derma of data which contains the core of a cultural unit—ideology, culture, philosophy, beliefs and history of societies.

The oral tradition has been a universal phenomenon, which carries the seed of the archetypal collective unconscious. Thus, this historical consciousness predates writing and continues to inspire writing generation after generation in diverse forms such as folklore, myths, legends, ballads, and fables.

The oral history and its transformation into text through folklore, carry the archetypes which provide patterns of universal parallels in thought systems of the world. They begin to bear resemblance to the "mono-myth" and have thematic parallels such as quest journeys, tragic heroes, chaste heroines, femme fatales, tales of love, and betrayal, tales of gods and demons, hunters, and dwarfs, etc.

In the Indian context, our aesthetic sensibilities have always been driven by '*Vak*' or the utterance, rather than by written language. The tradition of oral performance, in India has been ever old, ever new. However, the rich tradition of orality in India is marked by the challenge of variations in narratives on account of multiplicity of regional languages.

This work focuses on the oral literature related to king Vikramaditya, which resides in the collective memory and has so been transmitted collectively through generations one after the other.

The orality of the legendary king Vikramaditya has been recorded in several ancient texts, the most significant of the surviving ones include *Vetal Panchavimshati* and *Singhasan Battisi*. The legends contain the archetypal ethos and are evergreen, still manifesting themselves in hyper media and television serials and cartoons.

Most of the legends glorify the legendary ruler as a "*chakravarti samrath*" or a universal ruler, with his capital at Ujjain or in certain cases even in Pataliputra or Pratishthana. He is hailed as a great ruler who started a glorious new era—the *Vikram Samvat*, after defeating the Sakas.

Many attempts have been made to establish him as a historic person, born around the first century BCE. However, this stance is not free from several contradictions, the most glaring being that though Vikramaditya, the historical person is asserted to have existed around the first century BCE, yet the "*Vikram Samvat*", the era established by him begins after the 9th century CE.

The tales remember the legendary king as Vikramaditya or "the Sun of Valour". He is also referred to as Vikrama, Paramjit and Vikramarka (as *arka* also means the Sun). He is the hero who liberates his motherland India from the foreign invaders the so-called 'Mlechchha' or the 'Shakas'. He is also known by the epithet Shakari. In Jain legends, he is associated with another legendary king—Shalivahana of Pratishthana. In some of them, he is defeated by Shalivahana (who establishes the Shalivahana era) while in others, he is an ancestor of Shalivahana; a few legends also apply the title of Vikramaditya to the king of Pratishthana. The political rivalry between the two kings is sometimes also extended to patronage of language, with Vikramaditya supporting Sanskrit and Shalivahana supporting Prakrit.

The memory of the legendary king is etched in the collective memory of the Indian nation and Vikramaditya indisputably exists as a common title adopted by several Indian kings including the illustrious Chandragupta II. He serves as a standard and benchmark of valour and honour, to be awarded to those who emulate him as a role model and inculcate the qualities he stands for. Thus, while the evidence and existence of the legend from an objective historical standpoint would inevitably remain incomplete, Vikramaditya, the archetypal hero, has always lived and will continue to live.

Picture 2: Pingleshwar Mahadev, Ujjain

CHAPTER 3
Recreating Portraits with Archetypal Colours

3.1 The Archetypal Canvas: Genesis

The literary portrait of Vikramaditya has been sketched in this book on the generic canvas of the archetypal school of thought. The archetypal school of thought was among the most significant defining paradigms of the twentieth century. However, the school though still popular, has lost its former sheen in succession.

This chapter describes the genesis of the archetypal school of thought and explores the Indian association and influence on the development of the archetypal theory. The archetypal criticism was popularly introduced in literature largely by the Northrop Frye in his book *Anatomy of Criticism*, but it owes its genesis to the Swiss psychologist, Carl Gustav Jung.

During the early years of the twentieth century, Carl Jung, postulated the theory of the collective unconscious, and its contents, which he called the 'archetypes'. The collective unconscious was 'collective' rather than 'individual' indicating that the activity of the human mind was determined, not only from personal experience, but also from a super-personal, 'common Origin'.

C.G. Jung has an indelible place among the explorers of history of human consciousness. He introduced a mystical approach to psychology, which remains controversial. His ideas have cast a wide influence outside the scope of psychology spreading to arts, humanities, television, films, and society. His contribution to humanity's conception of itself in a collective sense has been significant. He believed that people should understand themselves in the context of meaning larger than themselves. No other modern psychologist seems have to integrated spirituality, philosophy, and religion with psychology as much as Jung did. His stance that the objective, empirical scientific thought cannot alone offer solace to the troubled human mind and the suffering Mankind is certainly idyllic, even though difficult to beget. He continues to inspire Jungians today to work out wide spread societal problems through a change in individual outlook, with the belief that an accumulation of individual changes will lead to a collective solution.

The story of Jung's ideas cannot begin without an introduction to the thought of his estranged comrade, Sigmund Freud. For many Freud and Jung would mean the world of psychology. They began as close comrades and Freud became not only a treasured colleague but also a father figure with whom Jung shared his soul. However, their friendship came to an end on account of intellectual differences. Yet, their theories, although different have, had the greatest impact on the perception of the human mind. Just as the opposites attract, complement and put together make, complete a whole; so, do Freud and Jung.

Freud's role in changing the way humanity perceived and dealt with mental illness is exceptional. Before Freud introduced psychoanalysis, mental illness was regarded 'organic' or was thought to occur due to physical degeneration or disease of the brain. Scores of psychologists treating patients were trying to discover the link between brain disease and insanity. In such a setting, Freud suggested that mental illness was caused by psychological factors, not physical factors, as widely assumed and developed psychoanalysis for treatment of his patients. Freud's most significant and popular concept, the model of the mind is outlined here.

Freud developed the topographical model of the mind, which is well known today, even outside the circles of psychology. He believed that human behaviour and personality were determined by the continuous interaction of conflicting psychological forces that operate at three different levels of awareness. He used the analogy of an iceberg and described the human mind as an arrangement of three components: the conscious mind, the preconscious mind and the unconscious mind (*Introduction to Psychology*, 1986).

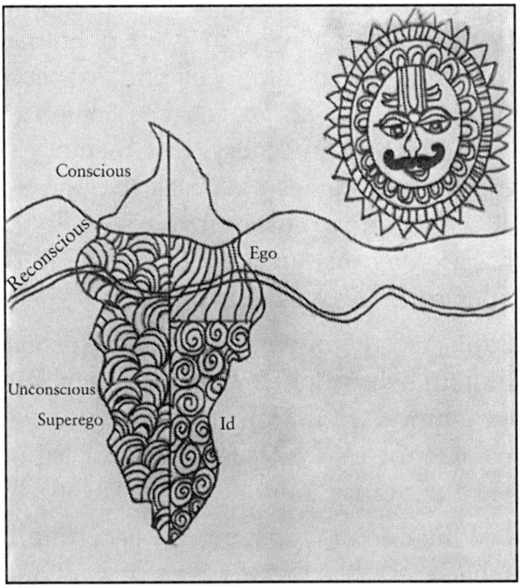

Picture 3: Freud's Topographical Model of the Mind

The *conscious mind* consists of all the mental processes (thoughts, feelings, memories, wishes, etc.) of which we are aware. For example, you may be feeling hungry at this moment and decide to order a pizza. This is seen as the tip of the iceberg, representing only a small portion, roughly ten per cent of the total working capacity of the mind. Just as the tip of the iceberg can be seen as it lies above water, we remain aware of this aspect of the mind.

At the second level lies the *preconscious mind*, which contains thoughts and feelings, that a person is not currently aware of, but which can easily be brought to consciousness. For example, you meet someone in the street whom you don't recognise instantly, but you slowly recollect his name and identity. This part lies submerged in water, but it is not buried deep enough and hence its contents can be accessed in due course.

At the third level lies the *unconscious mind*, which contains feelings, thoughts, urges, and memories that outside of our conscious awareness. Most of the contents of the unconscious are unacceptable or unpleasant, such as feelings of pain, anxiety, or conflict, which tend to govern human behaviour. For example, as child doesn't sing well and is often reprimanded by his school teacher. As he grows, he seems to 'forget' this unpleasant memory. But, in reality, this memory is not erased completely and lies buried deep beneath the layers of the mind. So, the child, who is now an adult, has developed stage fear. Thus, the unconscious memory which he apparently does not know, continues to influence his behaviour.

Freud established the unconscious as the primary source of influence of human behaviour (*Interpretation of Dreams*, 1990). But just as we cannot see the most critical and sizable bulk of an iceberg, we cannot easily access the most significant aspect of influence on the human mind.

The idea of the unconscious mind was certainly not Freud's invention and had existed in the philosophy, religion, and cultural traditions in both East as well as West. But its introduction, development, and popularity in clinical psychology are bound to Freud. He developed psychoanalysis to study the influences of the unconscious as manifesting in different ways, such as dreams.

Freud later developed a structural model of the mind, expressing it in terms of three functions: id, ego, and super-ego, which interact to determine the complex personality and behaviour of human beings.

The *id* is the most basic part of the human personality, and wants instant gratification of wants and needs. If these needs are not satisfied, a person becomes tense or anxious. The id lies in the unconscious part of the mind and responds directly to instincts, impulsively. For instance, if a person is very hungry and sees an apple, he will instantly consume it. Or, if there is a student who does not know the answer in the examination and feels compelled to cheat without giving a thought about the moral or ethical status of his conduct, merely acting on his impulse; he would be acting on impelled by his id. Freud held that a new born child's mind comprises id alone and the ego and super-ego develop only later. He also held that the id remains infantile in its function all through the life. As it lies within the unconscious part of the mind, it remains unaffected by time or experience. It involves primary process thinking marked by primitive, illogical, irrational, and fantasy-oriented thought process.

The *ego* develops from the id and ensures that the impulsive, unrealistic demands of id can be satisfied realistically in a socially acceptable manner. The ego is associated with secondary process thinking, which is rational, realistic, and orientated towards problem-solving. It is the decision-making part of the personality which weighs the pros and cons of an action and decides whether to act on an impulse or abandon it. For example, if a student appearing in an exam does not know the answer to a question, his id may provoke him to cheat, but his ego will weigh the norms of the society and check him from doing so. Ego is weaker than the adamant id and Freud compares the id to being a horse and the ego as its rider. The rider, who is rational should ideally direct the horse in the right direction. But at times the unreasonable, untameable horse can act on its instinct and refuse to follow the direction of the rider. So, in our example, the student provoked by the id to cheat, may override the instruction of the ego and cheat in the examination despite being directed towards the contrary. It should be noted that the ego too has no orientation of right or wrong, it simply seeks to mediate between the demands of the id and a realistically workable option. The concern of morally right or wrong behaviour falls within the zone of the super-ego, the third constituent of the model.

The *super-ego* is a repository of the moral standards and ideals, that we acquire from our parents and the society and thus constitutes our sense of right and wrong. It controls the id's impulses and acts as moral guide urging the ego to act upon idealistic rather than realistic principles.

In our illustration, if a student is provoked by the id to cheat, his ego will try to curtail his behaviour as it is not in accordance with the norms of the society, while his super-ego will instruct him not to do so on account of morally wrong conduct. But if the student does not abide by the instruction of the super-ego and cheats in the examination, the conscience which is a part of the super-ego will generate the feelings of guilt and remorse within the individual as a consequence. On the other hand, if the student doesn't cheat and develops an attitude of honesty, his ego ideal, the second part of super-ego may develop a feeling of pride. Also, if a person's conception of his ideal self is too high, then he may never feel satisfied with himself. The super-ego is present in the conscious, preconscious, and unconscious mind. The super-ego begins to develop around the age of three to five years.

Though the concept was developed by Freud in psychology, philosophical parallels to it have existed in ancient civilisations. Freud's structural model is comparable to Plato's tripartite soul philosophy. It is also comparable to the much broader and profound ambit of Yogic concepts such as *id* (prakriti), *aham* (ego), *mahattattva* (super-ego) and *chitta* (unconscious). His model is analogous to the model of *antahkaran* of the Advaita Vendanta school of Indian philosophy. It can also be assessed in light of the inciting soul, self-accusing soul, and contented soul of the Islamic philosophy.

Though these ideas were developed in scientific temper by Freud and his likes, they existed since times immemorial. The philosophical traditions of several ancient civilizations have also positioned the individual mind and soul in connection with the universal Mind and Soul; such as the idea of *jivatma* and *paramatma*, *purush*, and *virat purush*.

In the context of this background, Jung developed the theory of the collective unconscious. He reasoned that the complex behaviour of individuals, could not be a product of the individual's unconsciousness alone and linked it to the supra personal collective unconscious. Though he was Freud's most beloved comrade, yet he differed from Freud's theories on many counts. His intellectual differences with Freud led to their famous split, following which they parted ways.

Like Freud, Jung considered the psyche to be made up of separate but interacting systems including the ego and unconscious. But, unlike Freud, he asserted that the unconscious had two layers: the personal unconscious and the collective unconscious. He called the first layer, the *personal unconscious*, which is fundamentally the same as Freud's unconscious. The personal unconscious contains 'forgotten' information and repressed memories.

He called the second layer, the *collective unconscious*, which marks the most striking difference between Freud's theory and his own. The collective unconscious is the deepest layer of the unconscious, whose contents are common to entire mankind and which is shared by all beings of the same species. He further said that the contents of the collective unconscious are inherited and have never been a part of the conscious experience.

This assertion was perplexing to many as parts of what was conscious was supposed to be 'forgotten' and passed over to the unconscious. Then how could anything enter the unconscious without ever being a conscious experience first? Jung's mystic explanation was inherited common past of mankind.

Jung held that every man was born with universal predispositions stemming from a common ancestral past. The human mind carried an imprint of innate common characteristics just as the DNA carries the imprint of genetic instruction for a species. Since the collective unconscious is the deepest layer of the psyche, its contents remain largely inaccessible. But part of its contents, which Jung called *archetypes*, are manifested in the form of primordial images or thoughts, which have the same universal meaning, across different cultures.

The archetypes are expressed as symbols in literature, myth, folklore, sculpture, art, and in dreams. For example, the theme of victory of good over evil, the narratives of voyages especially across the sea are common to all cultures. When the archetype becomes conscious, it is expressed in myths and symbols, but gets coloured by the persona of the medium. Whether we come across Achilles fighting in the Trojan war for Helen or Rama battling in Lanka for Sita; Beowulf fighting Grendel or Sundiata fighting the sorcerer king Soumaoro Kante; the hero changes his garb to tell the same story in different names and narratives. Jung divided the archetypes into categories such as 'persona', 'shadow', 'self", 'anima', and 'animus', which are discussed later in the book.

Picture 4: Uma Mahesh, Bhanpura, Mandsaur, Ujjain

He believed that our shared primitive past continues to shape us in unknowing ways. These rudiments have been a constant companion to mankind in our journey through civilisations, casting their charms and charting our course. Jung's theory remains controversial in psychology and he has been criticised on many counts. Yet his place in psychology is well marked. His views have been born of many of his predecessors in the history of philosophical thought. His ideas have given birth to archetypal literary criticism. He shares his belief with of many of his kind, like a primordial thought itself.

Strong Son of God, immortal Love,
Whom we, that have not seen thy face,
By faith, and faith alone, embrace,
Believing where we cannot prove....
(*In Memoriam A.H.H.*—Lord Alfred Tennyson)

3.1.1 Archetypes: Snippets of Meaning

The archetypes are primordial patterns and universal images, that have existed since times immemorial. Emanating from the collective unconscious, the deepest layer of the psyche, they reveal knowledge that remains hidden from us in the conscious state. The ancient temples of India are replete with such images. Tibetan sacred art, Chinese temples, Buddhist monasteries and the Christian churches abound in these treasures. They live in myths, folklore, and fairy-tale. They are engraved in the animal art of the Palaeolithic caves, artefacts of early civilisations, in ancient paintings, art, and sculpture. Deep down they are etched in our memories and become accessible to every believing heart. These glorious images nurture the secrets of the soul in their breast. They reverberate the essence of God image to every discerning eye. They act as the transcendental bridge that connects the known to the unknown. These images buried among the shadows of our past carry glimpses of a revelation. They boost the spirit of selfhood and of universal brotherhood. They contain the seeds that make us One with ourselves and with our kind.

In the 1930s, Jung deployed the term archetypes in his famous Tavistock lecture and created a general fascination for the concept. Its scope enlarged immensely from psychology and spread to numerous fields like literature, music, painting, and sculpture. Maud Bodkin, Northrop Fry, and Joseph Campbell worked on the archetypes in literature and laid the foundation of archetypal literary criticism. The concept of the archetypes was not an original development by Jung and was an amalgamation of works of several scholars dating back to the works as early as those of Philo Judaeus and Irenaeus. However, the credit for its theorisation, application, and popularity inarguably belongs to Jung.

Jung examined empirical data and established the archetypes as inherited patterns of behaviour. He asserted that these archetypal images stemmed from the collective unconscious and were passed on from one generation to the other. Jung cited cases where ancient archetypal images recurred in the dreams of his patients, though they had never come across these images in their lives. They had never seen these images, yet they appeared in their dreams. This curious fact combined with Jung's experience as a child led him to his hypothesis. As a child, Jung remained preoccupied with a little manikin in whom he found profound meaning and power. He later identified it with stone images used as amulets of healing in Greek temples. Jung was not aware of these customs, yet as a child he imitated them.

To elucidate this point, Jung proposed an analogy to the birds building a nest. When the birds are engaged in building nests, they do not have a clear notion of exactly what they are involved in. But while they are not conscious of the nest-image, they do concentrate their efforts to build the nest that is identical to their species. Therefore, they do have the imprint of the archetypal nest of their species that guides them through their efforts.

Similarly, the archetypal image of the predator is encoded in the central nervous system of the ground nesting birds. In the 1930s, soon after Jung had proposed his analogy, several experiments were conducted on the behaviour of birds in the field of cognitive ethology, which are popularly known as Hawk/Goose effect. In one of the experiments, many generations of chicks were raised under controlled conditions and were not exposed to predators. However, when the ninth and the tenth generations of these chicks were introduced to a real or dummy hawk, they began to squirm and scamper. It was thus observed that the archetypal instinct of a species is an innate predisposition, which continues to affect its behaviour as long as the species continues to exist.

We may thus understand the Jungian archetypes as *an inherited pattern of behaviour or an innate predisposition, which emanates from the collective unconscious and is treasured as a universal treasure across all cultures.*

In his pursuit of the archetypes, Jung went beyond what empirical data and Western science could offer him. He approached several cultures voraciously plunging into abysmal depths of divinity in India, Taoist philosophy in China, and Christianity and Alchemy of the Western canon. He tirelessly explored myths and religious scriptures, trying to strike a meaningful connection. Many eminent thinkers across ages and across cultures had spoken of such ideas earlier.

Jung was influenced by the German philosopher, Friedrich Nietzsche and he analysed bits of Nietzsche's *Zarathustra* in many of his works. He regarded *Zarathustra* as an illustration of the prowess of the unconscious mind. Nietzsche is arguably most famous for his pessimistic critique of the European society, religious faith, and moral consciousness as well as for his audacious paradoxical pronouncement, "God is dead." Despite his controversial views, Nietzsche has remained one of the most influential and eloquent thinkers of the twentieth century. His admirers include Martin Heidegger, Michel Foucault, Thomas Mann, G.B. Shaw, W.B. Yeats, James Joyce, Jacques Derrida, Sigmund Freud, and Jean-Paul Sartre. Nietzsche's philosophy of "eternal recurrences" strikes a chord with Jung's ideas. In the August of 1881, Nietzsche was walking on the edge of Lake Silvaplana, near Surlej, when he came across a "pyramidal block of stone." He made a small note of this, reading "6,000 feet beyond man and time." This stone kindled the idea of the concept of eternal recurrence and provided the central theme of *Zarathustra*. Nietzsche has suggested that the eternal recurrence was his most important thought. A layperson may understand it as a proposition that all events repeat themselves in the same sequence through an eternal series of cycles. Nietzsche's ideas strike a chord with Jung's theory of archetypes and the unconscious. In order to substantiate his stance, Jung quotes Nietzsche in *Psychology of the Unconscious* in the following words:

> In our sleep and in our dreams we pass through the whole thought of earlier humanity. I mean, in the same way that man reasons in his dreams he reasoned when in the same

> state many thousands of years. (qtd. in *Psychology of the Unconscious*)

Rank, Riklin, and Abraham also share similar ideas whom Jung further quotes:

> Rank understands the myths in a similar manner, as a mass dream of the people. Riklin has insisted rightly upon the dream mechanism of the fables and Abraham has done the same for the myths. He says:
>
> "The myth is a fragment of the infantile soul life of the people," and "Thus, the myth is sustained, still remaining fragment from the infantile soul life of the people and the dream is the myth of the individual." (qtd. in *Psychology of the Unconscious*)

Among the precursors to archetypal thought, the name of Sir James George Fraser has secured a prominent place. He is credited as the first scholar to explicate the association between myths and rituals. Frazer's famous work, *The Golden Bough*, is an impressive collection of a wide variety of exotic beliefs and customs in relation to man's search for truth, knowledge, and control of his environment. Though his research methodology is rendered obsolete today and his work has attracted critics, yet his contribution to the field of social anthropology cannot be underscored. He introduced a comparative approach to study human social institutions. His work paved way for the birth and development of social anthropology. Frazer identified three stages in the development of the human psyche and placed them on a continuum: magical, religious, and scientific thought. The primitive society believed in magic and used it to appease nature and to control the environment. As centuries rolled, Man on accord of his mental advancement discredited magic and substituted it with religion to fill the gaps in his system of faith and security. With passing years and developing faculties, he embraced scientific thought and became a sceptic. In words of Frazer:

> By religion, then, I understand a propitiation or conciliation of powers superior to man which are believed to direct and control the course of nature and of human life. Thus

> defined, religion consists of two elements, a theoretical and a practical, namely, a belief in powers higher than man and an attempt to propitiate or please them. Of the two, belief clearly comes first, since we must believe in the existence of a divine being before we can attempt to please him. (*The Golden Bough*)

The development of human thought in civilisation mirrors the process of mental advancement in children. In their early childhood, little children are charmed by the magical fantasies, they are merrily enchanted by the tales of fairies and demons, gods, and goddesses. Their innocent minds do not raise doubts. As these children grow old, they learn to distinguish between imagination and reality. They soon transform into young adults who then look for observable facts before drawing conclusions.

Consider the faith of little children in Santa Clause. The mere mention of his name brings images of merry children, waiting excitedly to empty their stockings, looking for their presents arriving from the North Pole! We are all aware that the Santa Clause does not exist and the parents of the children are the actual benefactors. Still many parents love to indulge in this role-play with their children. Some of us probably are used to accepting the *specific givens* of our society. Since the Santa Clause is a social construct, it is accepted as a norm. There are few others who like to deviate from the norm; they may even ridicule the idea indulging in weighing the pros and cons of treating imagination over reality. Whatever be our stance, we can't deny that the Santa Clause has ensured his stay over time and has even increased his reach in terms of geographical spread. What is it that helped Santa endure through ages? Is it just the pleasant faced plum red old man with gifts ? Or is it something more? Why do little children living in places far away from Europe and USA smile to see the Santa even when they have nothing to do with Christianity? Are we to thank Coco Cola for its 1931 Christmas advertising campaign that took "Old Santa busiest man in the world" to different corners of the globe? Or is it something else?

The Santa Clause does not exist in reality. But the collective tradition of the people brings him to life. He does not exist as a person. But he exists as the spirit of loving benevolence, which makes the parents love their children and give them gracious presents without expecting anything in return. He is the recreation of Christ and serves as a constant reminder of the loving benevolence of Christ's sacrifice for Mankind. It is this principal of a parent's unconditional love for his children behind the facade of the Santa that has endured the test of time.

Picture 5: Hindola Toran, Gyaraspur, Vidisha

The little children can feel the spirit of the Santa due to their enhanced perceptibility in early childhood. But as they

it because when children grow, they don't like to be called by their nicknames? They hate their childhood games because they think they have grown old. They may deny but they can't falsify that their childhood shaped them and made them what they are today. They deserve to be excused. For they didn't realise that what they do today is linked to their past. And so, for every corrective action that they may want to take today, they will have to recall their past.

But most of us like to live in the present. Some of us may agree now that the past is important but may become sceptical about what to trust? The historical accounts being productions of the past are filtered through the persona of the medium, the writer. To what extent this medium approaches reality remains questionable. His account may be coloured by personal tastes and subject to the individual's limitations.

Virginia Woolf has raised doubts on the skills of historians regarding authentic documentation of past histories in her work *Orlando*. She suggests that in this task the historian tends to mix reality with his own imagination. The feud between reality and imagination or truth and beauty seems eternal. Seers and philosophers have solved this paradox by referring to it as two sides of the same coin. The dictum *Satyam Shivam Sundaram* echoes this idea, which the poet John Keats borrowed and declared, "Beauty is truth, truth beauty,—that is all, Ye know on earth, and all ye need to know." Emily Dickinson also suggests the same idea in her poem, "I Died for Beauty but was Scarce"—

> He questioned softly why I failed?
> "For beauty," I replied.
> "And I for truth,—the two are one;
> We brethren are," he said.
> (Emily Dickinson, "I Died for Beauty but was Scarce")

The cohesion of imagination and reality culminates into the greatest synthesis of genius. The German organic chemist, August Kekulé, was working on the molecular structure of benzene for years with much success. Almost as he had begun to lose hope, he had a dream experience in which he saw six chains of carbon and hydrogen atoms turning to form circles resembling snakes biting their tails. He instantly grasped that the benzene molecule must be composed of six carbon atoms bound to one another in a ring. His discovery laid the foundation of the theory of chemical structure. The structure resembled 'Ouroboros', a symbol originating in ancient Egyptian iconography, which was adopted by the Greek magical tradition, Renaissance magic, Gnosticism, Hermeticism, alchemy, and modern symbolism. It represents the eternal return or cyclicality. Kekulé understood this and acknowledged that he had made an organic as well as a scientific discovery. When he presented his findings at a conference, he said: "Let us learn to dream, gentlemen, and then we may perhaps find the truth."

Kekulé had dreamt of the 'Ouroboros', a symbol of a serpent biting its tail. It represents the eternal cyclic renewal in life and the universe. We are aware of biochemical cycles like the water cycle, carbon cycle, or the nitrogen cycle in which a chemical substance passes through the biotic and abiotic components of the Earth and returns back to the same starting point. This cycle goes on repeating, renewing the resources and making their sustenance possible for the future.

The 'Ouroboros' logically proposes the same idea; rebirth after death continues eternally, both individually and universally. The mathematical symbol of infinity that we use today is believed to come from another version of the Ouroboros a double-looped serpent eating its tail.

The idea of 'Ouroboros' is common across several cultures. It was worshipped by the ancient Egyptians as a symbol of the sun. It was then borrowed by the Phoenicians and passed on to the Greek who named it 'Ouroboros' or tail devourer. The alchemical textbook, *Chrysopoeia of Cleopatra* contains a drawing of the ouroboros representing it as half-light and half-dark, echoing the union of opposites such as the conscious and the unconscious and the Chinese Yin and Yang. The words "ἕν τό πᾶν" meaning "one is all", are written in the picture. The double-looped serpent also reflects the same unison of duality through the two loops. It resonates the idea of primordial unity of the universe starting from the primordial chaos and ending in it only to be born again.

It is depicted in myths and legends of several countries. The Norse legend about serpent 'Jormungand', who guarded the Tree of Life and grew so large that it encircled the entire world and grasped its tail in its teeth, resonates the image of 'Ouroboros'.

The image of the serpent with its tail in its mouth encircling the world turtle, or the Kurma of Hindu mythology connotes the same idea. Different versions of this myth are found in India, China, and North America. The serpent is associated with 'desire' in many texts including the Bible. The withdrawal of the tortoise into his shell shields him from the serpent Desire and enables him to channelize his energy towards his spiritual destination, the mount Meru. The *Bhagvad Gita* 2/58 reads:

> "*yada samharate cayam kurmo 'nganiva sarvasah indriyanindriyarthebhyas tasya prajna pratisthita*".
>
> (The one who is able to withdraw his senses from sense objects, as the tortoise draws its limbs within the shell, is to be understood as truly situated in knowledge.)

The comforting image of baby Krishna, sucking the thumb of his foot, floating on a *vatpatra* (banyan leaf) on the waters of universal deluge soothingly reciprocates the eternal cyclic renewal of life. The divine innocence of baby Krishna radiates the idea not with heavy words of wisdom but with the happy taste of sublime sweetness.

In 1913, the Dutch physicist, Niels Bohr had conceptualised the model of the atom after a dream in which he envisioned the planets spinning around him. Upon waking, he went to his lab to test the idea, which lead to the conception of the structure of the atom with the electrons circling around the nucleus. He received the Nobel Prize for physics in 1922 for his contribution to the theory of atomic structure and quantum theory.

Until the 1920s, diabetes was considered a fatal disorder which had no cure. The patients suffering from the disease were put on a diet low on carbohydrates and sugar and high in fat and protein. The number of years they had for survival after the diagnosis were limited. Dr Frederick Banting and Charles Best were committed towards finding a cure for diabetes. During the course of his work, Banting had a dream urging him to surgically tie up the pancreas, so as to stop the flow of insulin. He tested this idea and observed an imbalance between blood sugar and insulin. Banting and Best worked with their research team to purify insulin for treating diabetic patients. What would have happened had these men discarded their dreams?

Another illustration, which comes to my mind is the game of Snakes and Ladders, a game that most of us would have played as children. A game with a hundred square blocks, where we start from the number one and try to reach hundred, the snakes pushing us down and ladders helping us up. A game ruled by the throw of the dice, not so much by our skills but still has managed popularity through the ages.

The origin of the game can be traced back to ancient times and it is believed to be created by a poet-saint, Gyandev to serve as an aid to moral instruction. The original game was then known as *mokshpat* or *mokshapath* (path to salvation) and *paramapadam* (supreme abode). The task of the player was to start from 1 and reach the number 100, which represented God or complete self-realisation. The snake—evil deeds or vices created an obstacle in the path of moral progress and brought them down. Ethical deeds and thoughts took them up the ladders to sub heavens like the *brahmaloka*, *kailasa* and *vaithuntha*. The number of ladders related to virtues or rewards are believed to be only four while the punishments were much more in comparison hinting at the idea that while too many try to reach the designated heaven, only a few succeed. It is believed that the ladders were found on numbers, 12, 51, 57, 76, and 78 representing faith, reliability, generosity, knowledge, and asceticism respectively. The snakes were found on numbers 41, 44, 49, 52, 58, 62, 69, 73, 84, 92, 95, and 99 symbolising disobedience, arrogance, vulgarity, theft, lying, drunkenness, debt, murder, anger, greed, pride, and lust respectively. The squares were also interspersed with pictures of animals, plants and similar objects of symbolic significance.

As centuries rolled on, the British adopted this fascinating game and spread it in Victorian England. The cultural adaptation was inevitable though. The Hindu morality changed its garb and attuned to the Christian virtues and vices. The overall conception still remained unchanged. The game became popular. Soon, beautiful, colourful glossy boards appeared ornate with exquisite art doing away with the instruction in morality. The essential theme of serpents punishing evil deeds bringing them down and the ladders rewarding the good deeds taking them up has been retained to our day.

With the advent of online games, Snakes and Ladders may assume a new guise or may even slowly turn into a relic. The transformation of Snakes and Ladders from a game of moral instruction to its new form shows us that the archetypal image of the snake conveys the essence of the game even now when the blank squares have been washed of their meaning.

The archetypal images, like Snakes and Ladders stand as souvenirs of the past, washed of their meaning. Their presence bears a testimony to the absence.

Like the game of Snakes and Ladders, the archetypal images, have been washed of their meaning over the centuries. They do however retain their own essence in their structure and in their being.

We experience the unconscious through symbols encountered in all aspects of life: dreams, art, religion, and other pursuits of life. We come across archetypes all around us. But we flow in the flux of a 'negative affirmation' along with our fellowmen in a customary denial of the affirmative. We all have moments of ambivalent 'denied acceptance'. The theme of 'good over evil' is a common feature in the mythic tradition in almost every culture.

It can be logically accepted that good is better than evil in most cases and for most people. However, how many of them have never entertained an evil thought or never committed an evil deed? We differ only in degrees not in kind. Few would accept that they are afraid in the dark, more will react when the lights go out. The behaviour is justified as who can see the unseen?

Know the unknown? But the 'accepted' already lies buried deep. Understanding the conscious better than unconscious is natural. Moving with time rather than regression into past is most desirable. Understanding the archetype, as most comprehend, is not dwelling in the deep dark past. It is realignment of the past with present, which Jung calls 'individuation' that would result in a clear, comprehensive, consolidated flow of thought.

Jung borrowed substance from the Eastern philosophy, alchemy, astrology, sociology, as well as literature and the arts. He cautioned against the skewed proclivity of the modern humanity to rely too heavily on science and logic and advocated a more balanced view that would integrate unconscious realm.

Not many psychologists support Jung today. Institutions providing training in Jungian therapeutics remain scarce. Jungian theory is not a part of the curriculum in the psychology stream in most of the educational institutions; it is however incorporated in the humanities occasionally. Yet, we cannot deny his contribution to psychology. Perhaps, his absence is his real presence. The crux of Jung's theory is mystic in character. The mystic philosophy is beyond words, logic, argument, and attestation. It can only be felt, not seen or proved. Jung's invisible ideas remain largely unseen by Psychology which demands proof. In the 1940s and 1950s, the Jungian influence on literature incited the critics like Northrop Frye and Maud Bodkin leading to the formulation of archetypal criticism. It continues to inspire us till date.

However, it is paradoxical that while the theory remains rather unscientific for psychology, it is somewhat a little too scientific for literature. An assessment of the archetype is like approaching a beautiful monsoon morning to make an estimate about precipitation and humidity. By doing this, one can gather everything except the inherent beauty of the moment. The soulful beauty of the archetype can never be understood completely unless we tie the mind and heart together. For the archetype, is not to scrutinised, analysed and dissected. Chopping them into bits and pieces will drain them out of their essence. The resolution perhaps lies in reverence. The archetype is to be beheld in splendour. It is to be venerated in the blissful glory of *sat chitt ananda*. It is to be approached with the curious eyes of an innocent child filled with awe and wonder, not with the enquiring perusal of an investigator. Such a humanist approach towards the archetype can unravel it in a richer, fuller light. The mystics in literature seem to have reverberated these ideals eternally.

The universal essence of the archetype can best be felt in literature. The Indian poet seer, Rabindranath Tagore advocated an approach of universal humanism culminating from his *Upanishadic* vision upholding that the core values of all cultures should bond Men together into a peaceful brotherhood. Almost all students of Indian schools sing Tagore's prayer *Where the Mind is Without Fear*, seeking the 'heaven', "where the world has not been broken up into fragments by narrow domestic walls." In "Unending Love", he sings:

> Whenever I hear old chronicles of love, its age-old pain,
> Its ancient tale of being apart or together.
> As I stare on and on into the past, in the end you emerge,
> Clad in the light of a pole-star piercing the darkness of time:
> You become an image of what is remembered forever.
> You and I have floated here on the stream that brings from the fount.
> At the heart of time, love of one for another.
> We have played alongside millions of lovers, shared in the same
> Shy sweetness of meeting, the same distressful tears of farewell—
> Old love but in shapes that renew and renew forever.
>
> Today it is heaped at your feet, it has found its end in you
> The love of all man's days both past and forever:
> Universal joy, universal sorrow, universal life.
> The memories of all loves merging with this one love of ours—And the songs of every poet past and forever.
> (Tagore, "Unending Love")

The healing power of the soothing images in literature can act as a balm for the "broken, fragmented world" of our day and can contribute however imperceptibly to strike down the "narrow domestic walls."

The image of dancing, golden daffodils which reminded Wordsworth of the Milky Way, is distinctively known to have restored him to tranquillity in his "pensive mood":

> I wandered lonely as a cloud
> That floats on high o'er vales and hills,
> When all at once I saw a crowd,
> A host, of golden daffodils; Beside
> the lake, beneath the trees,
> Fluttering and dancing in the breeze.
> Continuous as the stars that shine
> And twinkle on the Milky Way,
> They stretched in never-ending line
> Along the margin of a bay:
> Ten thousand saw I at a glance,
> Tossing their heads in sprightly dance.
>
> The waves beside them danced, but they
> Out did the sparkling waves in glee:
> A Poet could not but be gay,
> In such a jocund company:
> I gazed—and gazed—but little thought
> What wealth the show to me had brought:
>
> For oft, when on my couch I lie
> In vacant or in pensive mood,
> They flash upon that inward eye
> Which is the bliss of solitude;
> And then my heart with pleasure fills,
> And dances with the daffodils.
> (Wordsworth, Daffodils)

But while the golden daffodils restored Wordsworth to tranquillity, they stirred Jamaica Kincaid's Lucy out of tranquillity, in the post-colonial times. When Lucy was forced to learn the poem *Daffodils*, which was about a flower alien to her land, she made daffodils a symbol of brutal colonialism. She conjured the tranquil image as "a scene of conquered and conquests; a scene of brutes masquerading as angels and angels portrayed as brutes."

The naivest objects can convey different meanings to different people in different times. If we employ archetypes or the universal symbols that convey universal meaning to people of different cultures living in diverse spatial and temporal frames, we may fill in the gaps. They can go a long way in augmenting a multicultural curriculum for the new age student of a global world. These patterns of our common past are a universal heritage that seeks our attention and protection. But, unfortunately, just like countless ancient monuments they stand in ruins unattended.

3.1.3 The Collective Unconscious

Once upon a time in midwinter, when the snowflakes were falling like feathers from heaven, a queen sat sewing at her window, which had a frame of black ebony wood. As she sewed she looked up at the snow and pricked her finger with her needle. Three drops of blood fell into the snow. The red on the white looked so beautiful that she thought to herself, "If only I had a child as white as snow, as red as blood, and as black as the wood in this frame."

Soon afterward she had a little daughter who was as white as snow, as red as blood, and as black as ebony wood, and therefore they called her Little Snow-White. And as soon as the child was born, the queen died.

A year later the king took himself another wife. She was a beautiful woman, but she was proud and arrogant, and she could not stand it if anyone might surpass her in beauty. She had a magic mirror. Every morning she stood before it, looked at herself, and said:

Mirror, mirror, on the wall,
Who in this land is fairest of all?

To this the mirror answered:

> You, my queen, are fairest of all.
>
> Then she was satisfied, for she knew that the MIRROR SPOKE THE TRUTH.

Snow-White grew up and became ever more beautiful. When she was seven years old, she was as beautiful as the light of day, even more beautiful than the queen herself.

One day when the queen asked her mirror:

> Mirror, mirror, on the wall,
>
> Who in this land is fairest of all?

It answered:

> You, my queen, are fair; it is true.
>
> But Snow-White is a thousand times fairer than you.

This is how the story "Little Snow-White" by the Brothers, Jacob and Wilhelm Grimm begins. Disney animators spread the fairy-tale to different parts of the world where it lives in different flavours. We come across similar legendary narratives in almost all cultures such as the German, Scottish, Swiss, Italian, Greek, Albanian, and Russian.

In the allegorical Indian epic poem "Padmawat", queen Nagamati asks her parrot, "Who is more beautiful, I or Padmawati?" But the parrot SPOKE THE TRUTH and replied to her displeasure. In the Armenian fairy-tale, every month, the woman asks the new moon, "Am I the most beautiful in the world, or are you?". Each month the moon duly replies, "You are most beautiful." Soon after her beautiful daughter Nourie Hadig is born and blossoming. So, when she puts up the question to the moon, who SPOKE THE TRUTH, and this time he replies, "Nourie Hadig is more beautiful than you or I". Kristen Stewart's *Snow White and the Huntsmen* puts the tale in a new frame. Anne Sexton sings of the tale in *Snow White and the Seven Dwarfs*:

> Meanwhile Snow White held court, rolling her china-blue doll eyes open and shut and sometimes referring to her mirror as women do.

These legends from around the world are tied with a common chord. Whether it is the mirror, the moon or the parrot, they all SPEAK THE TRUTH. They strip of the cover, the persona, the mask of the actor, the "beauty" that we "see" and reveal the true face of the SELF hidden behind the deep dark layers of the unconscious. Jung has tied such similar but scattered tit-bits of mythology and art into a cohesion through his theory of the collective unconscious.

Psychology studies the psyche, the sum of the human mind, conscious, and the unconscious. We make sense of the world around us through the interplay of these faculties. We may come across external objects which we perceive it externally by our sense organs and conscious awareness.

The Yogic philosophy also states that, our *Buddhi* is directed externally, towards sense objects. It is the tendency of the *Buddhi* to get attached to external objects, so when the sense perceive objects which we 'like', we become attached and want to possess things; and it is this tendency of the buddhi, which is extremely hard to overcome and gives birth to desires, which become the cause of suffering. However, the Buddhi also has another aspect called *Viveka*, the faculty of discriminative intelligence, which can direct this process. Yoga suggest that possessing objects will are a need is not wrong. However, desiring objects, creating attachments, and wanting to possess things, is certainly undesirable behaviour.

Jung's theory views psyche as being made up of interacting systems. The primary ones are the conscious mind (ego), the personal unconscious and collective unconscious. The conscious mind or the Ego is made of thoughts, memories, and emotions that a person is aware of. But just as we store a lot of data in a computer but save the bulk in the hard disk and retain only what is required for immediate operation in the random-access memory; so does our mind retain only a fraction of its contents in the conscious mind and transfers the rest to the personal unconscious. The personal unconscious thus acts as a storehouse of temporarily forgotten thoughts and repressed memories. It is inevitable that the personal unconscious owes its existence to the conscious experience. Thus, whatever is there in the personal unconscious is first experienced in the conscious state and then filtered and passed down to the personal unconscious. It is thus an exclusive personal acquisition and contains nothing that is a part of heredity. For instance, consider a young student who is not good in sports and frequently get thrashed by his trainer. As the student matures, he 'forgets' this unpleasant experience and moves on in life. However, this experience 'forgotten' by the conscious mind is actually pushed to reside in his personal unconscious. Even when years pass and the child now an adult plays a sport, the unseen, unpleasant memory buried in his unconscious makes him a diffident player. But if the adult can locate and erase this childhood memory, the game is his!

The psyche composed of the conscious mind and the unconscious mind as expressed above was acknowledged by the contemporaries of Jung, significantly by Freud. Jung further asserted that the unconscious is composed of not one but two layers: the personal unconscious and the collective unconscious. The contents of the collective unconscious are not a personal acquisition and had never been present in consciousness. They are universally inherited behaviour traits of a *priori existence.* The assertion made by Jung became highly contentious as it put forth a perplexing issue: how could anything be present in the unconscious, without initial screening in the conscious? It sounded as absurd to people as finding something in the computer hard disk, which was never given as an input to the computer.

However, the human mind is not a machine. The computer works on the principle of garbage in and garbage out but the human mind can create useful objects from waste material. Jung convincingly augmented his assertion through the case studies of his patients and more substantially by drawing universal parallels between mythology, literature, philosophy, and art from different countries and cultures. The Jungians today sustain the theory by a corresponding analogy with the DNA (deoxyribonucleic acid) that codes genetic information for the transmission of inherited traits.

The best examples of expression of the collective unconscious are the universal parallels in myth, legend and folk-lore throughout the world such as the theme of victory of good over evil which appears as a motif in the myths of most cultures since times immemorial when communication across borders was limited. Since the very nature of the phenomenon is collective, not individual, therefore, logically it can be best appreciated at a macro level. However, to examine the phenomenon at an individual level, let us consider a person who dreams of a strange ritual which he has never experienced in his life, i.e. through his conscious self and later comes to know that the ritual is a part of tribal customs of the aboriginals of Australia then such a memory, which has never been in his personal conscious and so is not personally acquired will be attributed to the inherited pattern of his collective unconscious, which stores his species specific information just like the DNA stores the genetic code. Jung had actually come across patients with such an experience linked to the universal parallels in myth and mythology of different parts of the world and he used his extensive knowledge to cure them. Many of us would agree that Jung was more of a mystic than a psychologist and for that reason he perhaps remains closer to literature than psychology.

Jung asserted that the collective unconscious, the deeper, collective layer of the psyche, was made up of *archetypes*. The *archetype* is the content of the collective unconscious. It is the inherited pattern of instinctual behaviour identical in all men and present in each one of us. The archetypes are projected by the collective unconscious in the conscious but they most often fail to reach the consciousness completely. They are manifested in the conscious in the form of dreams and myths.

The archetype is thus an inherited pattern independent of personal conscious influence and collective conscious and culture. The supra-personal nature of the archetypes of the collective unconscious makes their diagnosis a daunting task, as it is not easy to ascertain the extent and influence of conscious elements. The unconscious elements may be derived from conscious experience and personal acquisitions. Cryptomnesia or the condition when a forgotten memory returns without being recognized by the subject is to be ruled out.

The most challenging task may be the practitioner's in-depth understanding of world mythology. Logically, too, if understanding the unconscious, the submerged layer of the psyche is difficult, then comprehending the collective unconscious a layer further deep will be further tricky. The inherent complexity of the collective unconscious has delimited its scope in the psychoanalytic circles. Jungian thought has even been refuted at times by psychoanalytic critics. There seems to be a paucity of concrete categorical models in support of the stance in psychology. But the theory entails a staunch support from mythology and literature, from which it scrounges endearingly.

The Jungian theory can be counted as a weighty contestant of one of the oldest arguments in the history of psychology, the nature versus nature debate. The squabble seems eternal involving the clash of ideas of Plato and Aristotle in 350 BC, to Immanuel Kant and John Locke during the Enlightenment period, to the pondering of Mary Shelly in her novel *Frankenstein*, and extends right up to the 'naturalists' and 'nurturists' of our time. John Locke's philosophy of *tabula rasa*, that holds that the human psyche is like a "blank slate" on which anything can be written suggesting that the human beings are moulded and nurtured by their environment rather than by their innate tendency towards showing a specific behaviour. His ideas are in sync with the empiricist dictum of Aristotle, "*Nihil est in intellectu quod non prius in sensu*" (knowledge arises from evidence gathered via sense experience). The modern theory of behaviourism is rooted in this empiricist view.

Jungian thought supports the stance that a person is born with an innate nature or an *a priori* disposition which governs his behaviour apart from the way he was nurtured in the environment. The Greek philosopher Plato also believed that behaviour and knowledge accrue from innate factors. The Prussian philosopher Kant, also believed that before the mind can comprehend and make sense of any experience, an *a priori* structure should be 'pre-present' to make the comprehension possible. The famous anthropologist, Francis Galton showed in his research that intelligence is inherited by heredity, in his work *Natural Intelligence* (1889), favouring the nature side of the debate. The French philosopher Rene Descartes asserted that all individuals possess in-born ideas that govern their approach to the world. William Golding's *Lord of the Flies* puts forth the idea that human beings are born with an innate predisposition towards evil. Jung's ideas thus have their own niche in the great tradition. Many great thinkers coming both before and after him have shared the same stream of thought.

There are conceptual equivalents of Jung's theory of collective unconscious and the Vedic thought, some of which Jung has illustrated and acknowledged in several of his works. The Vedic sages had perceived unity between the self and Universal selves. Some scholars interpret the collective unconscious as a diminutive of the numerous aspects of Brahman, the highest Universal Principle of major schools of Hindu philosophy. *Brihadaranyaka Upanisad* upholds *aham brahma asmi* (I am Brahman) and hints at the presence of the Universal soul in individual soul. Tagore sings of the same in *Geetanjali*:

> I shall ever try to drive all evils away from my heart and keep my love in flower, knowing that thou hast thy seat in the inmost shrine of my heart.
>
> True, whoever looks into the mirror of the water will see first of all his own face. Whosoever goes to himself risks a confrontation with himself. The mirror does not flatter; it faithfully shows whatever looks into it; namely the face we never show to the world because we cover it with the persona, the mask of the actor. But the mirror lies behind the mask and shows the true face. (C.G. Jung, *Archetypes of the Collective Unconscious*)

3.2 Archetypal Paints: Recollections of a Literary Legacy

The archetypal paradigm permeated literature and arose as a movement beginning in early 1930s and outspreading through the remainder of the decade, developing a new approach towards literary exploration accomplished by the study of recurrent patterns in literary divisions such as plot, character and themes which signify universal common human experience. Apart from the work of C.G. Jung in psychology, the movement rests upon the effort of his predecessor, the Scottish anthropologist, Sir James Frazer. His monumental book, *The Golden Bough* tracked the origin of myth to prehistoric practices and flagged the way for the development of archetypal thought. The Cambridge School of Comparative Anthropology, including scholars like Gilbert Murray, Jane Harrison, and Andrew Lang, drew inspiration from Frazer. In 1920, Jessie Weston published her book, *From Ritual to Romance*, which is best, reminisced as an inspiration to T.S. Eliot for the *Wasteland*.

The introduction of the term archetype in literary criticism is ascribed to Maud Bodkin, who published her thesis, *Archetypal Patterns in Poetry* in 1934. Her study investigated literary motifs that typified "eternal durability" appearing in "plot patterns" and "character types." She is accredited for having presented the literary technique of "splitting" of "type figures" which she illustrated through the illustration of Hamlet and its analogical parallel Oedipus. She expounded the archetypal rebirth motif through an examination of *The Ancient Mariner* and emphasized patterns of universal recurring themes and images in selected texts of poetry. She held that the function of poetry is the proposition of offering an "integrated *Weltanschauung*" to the human community. She is fondly acknowledged as a pioneer in the field of archetypal literary criticism.

Another archetypal critic, William Troy, deserves a mention, whose works primarily rely on scattered articles published in notable journals. He endorsed the archetypal "type figures" in literature suggested by Bodkin. Though his research techniques are regarded more objective than Bodkin's by some critics, history has been kinder to Bodkin, in terms of popular appeal.

As an addition to the "type figures", a new literary dimension was introduced in the archetypal stream by Lord Raglan. He developed a checklist of twenty-two points elucidating the points of distinction between a "myth hero" and a "historic hero". He classified the groups further into three categories: cultural rites conducted at birth, initiation into society, and death.

The archetypal critics in the initial phase were essentially involved in the task of developing typological groups based on patterns of observation of literary universal parallels and were lacking in essence in terms of scientific and objective methodology.

However, the Canadian literary critic, Northrop Frye, burst afresh the convention and his publication, *Anatomy of Criticism* (1957) became the founding text of archetypal literary criticism. He enlarged the scope of archetypal criticism following an analytic schema and introduced objectivity resulting in advancement from what had been historic, comparative, typological study of fiction till then; towards becoming a scientific, analytic, and interpretative study. Frye attacked the New Critics who advocated microscopic linguistic analysis and regarded individual texts as self-contained units. He combated the application of critical theories existing outside literature and advocated the: "examination of literature in terms of a conceptual frame-work derivable from an inductive survey of the literary field" (Frye, 7). He considers archetypes as associative clusters, which can be communicated due to a sizeable number of people within the culture being acquainted with them.

He developed the "theory of modes" dividing literature into five modes from a historically oriented critical perspective: 'mythic', 'romantic', 'high mimetic', 'low mimetic', and 'ironic'; each period being linked to, though not rigidly to, a specific historical period; and established cyclical relations between the periods. He delineated the categories based upon the relativity of the protagonist's position successively degeneration in each successive period. The protagonist in the mythic mode, is a larger-than-life character like a God or a supernatural being and the narrative is essentially supra-literary. The consecutive period, termed romantic mode, encompasses legends and folk tales. The protagonist, in this mode is a mortal of high social rank endowed with lofty qualities superior distinctive from other characters and the setting in general. The third period termed high mimetic mode, includes traditional categories of epic and tragedy. The protagonist in this mode is a leader superior to the other characters but not to his environment. The fourth category, the low mimetic mode, which particularly includes irony and realistic fiction, puts the protagonist at par, or even at a relatively inferior position in comparison to other characters and the environment.

Frye's "theory of modes" can be regarded as an extension of the "historical types of figures" developed by his literary ancestors. However, he extended the scope of archetypal criticism, if we may so call it, given Frye's assertion of points of distinction between the Jungian and literary archetypes; by introducing analytic schema for the syntactic analysis of the texts through: literal, allegorical, moral, and anagogic meaning formulation. The archetypes are inter-textually connected, in the anagogic phase, and offers a transcendent glimpse of literature as an independent, autonomous, self-creating 'order of words'.

In the archetypal context, he suggested treating an individual text as a small subset of the entire body of literature, with the aim of deriving structural patterns through recurrent patterns of observation. He identified "four pre-generic elements of literature" which he termed "mythoi" or "generic plots," and grouped them in two opposed pairs. In his essay, *Rhetorical Criticism: Theory of Genres*, he delineated generic distinctions of literature as archetypes of convention. Frye's contribution to archetypal criticism has substantially become its structure and substance.

The mythologist Joseph Campbell is another influential writer associated with this field. The magnitude of his work is extensive spanning several cultures across the world. He applied the principles of Jungian psychology to arrive at his notion of the 'monomyth' in his most notable work, *The Hero with a Thousand Faces*. He studied the myths of several cultures throughout the world and discerned patterns of universal parallels in these. These 'hero myths' displayed fundamentally similar pattern of departure or separation, initiation, and return. In these myths, the hero is typically born in a 'mysterious' or a 'miraculous' manner and typically spends his childhood with surrogate parents. He is mentored by "an old wise master" towards accomplishing training or education. He is then led to 'a quest for identity', often towards fulfilling a special duty; through which he discovers his virtues and weaknesses, and through an apotheosis develops his superior Self. The journey either advances towards a higher spiritual realm along with a 'return'; or a descent into darkness with a 'return'. The saga is metaphorically comprehended as the Soul's spiritual journey through different births towards a better self; or the self's psychic journey towards individuation; shared and narrated through the collected memory of all cultures.

Campbell's work shares closer quarters with myth than with criticism; but the overall temper of archetypal criticism itself, nearly, is as such. As most literary theories bend, break and fade in time, the popularity of archetypal literary criticism began to fade in the influx of critical post-modern perspectives. Frye and Jung have both been criticized by post-modern critics, but their theory, though not so fashionably in, still remains a steady tool of literary analysis.

In an Indian context, it may be pertinent that, archetypal literary criticism was booming and bustling in the West when, India was struggling for freedom and later grappling with social problems. By the time Indian literary critics took up pens, the theory had passed out of fashion. In this sense, this theory has been largely unexplored, with respect to 'Indian Writings in English'. However, the approach bears strong affinity with the Indian soil as acknowledged by Jung himself and as illustrated by Joseph Campbell in works on Oriental myths. Many of the ancient Indian works written in Sanskrit literature are characterised by parallel 'type' classifications such as that of an 'ideal woman'; which the archetypal critics termed 'type figures'. Thus, the saga of archetypal criticism holds good for research on ancient Indian texts and starts afresh, ever old, ever new.

Picture 6: Vishnu's Leviathan Avatar Trimipramine, 12th century AD, City Palace Museum, Jaipur

Chapter 4
Rebirth of a Legend

4.1 Vetaal Panchavimshati: An Archetypal Reading

The literary narrative of king Vikramaditya is more mythic than historic. The chronicles which mention and recollect the king are numerous yet varied and present details which are contradictory and perplexing. It thus follows that we remember the great king as a cultural icon rather historical person.

However, it is understandable that the narrative of Vikramaditya has been modified through its retellings over successive generations and decoding the original message in terms of its entirety, content, and intention is an unworkable task. However, the subliminal aspects of any literature which can stand the test of time, in terms of its successive handling down through ages, are evidently not inherent in factual details but accrue from a universal applicability and relevance.

The literary projection of Vikramaditya's image in myths accrues from a stable source which has sustained its successive transmission, even though with severe dilution of the actual message and content. However, beneath the layers of illusionary apparatus lies buried the core of truth, deeply hidden, and concealed.

The tendency of the contemporary narrative to be written in the genre of the semblance of mystery and miracle plays, with possibly didactic intentions has rendered their logical comprehension nearly impossible. The *Vetaal Panchavimshati* is a popular text which narrates the story of Vikramaditya with elements of the fantastic and super-natural. The story of what can be seen a spiritual quest or a modern 'bildungsroman-ical' transformation of a king is narrated through a typical narrative with a riddled structure. This section attempts to uncover the *Vetaal Panchavimshati* through critical analyses.

Vetaal Panchavimshati is compilation of tales and legends written in Sanskrit. However, the tales are a compilation based on oral literature of much older historical past. They have been drawn from the narratives of the mysterious *Brihat Katha*, authored by Gunadhya, in the esoteric language Pishachi, which is now lost.

Gunadhya's *Brihat Katha* cast a great influence on literature of the succeeding literary periods and his tales survived through oral tradition, even though the original manuscript was lost. The literary Raja Bhoja acknowledged the *Brihat Katha* as a class of literature in itself.

The earliest available and the most notable renditions of *Vetaal Panchavimshati,* a part of the *Brihat Katha*, in Sanskrit, comprise the works of two Kashmiri poets. The first being Somadeva, who compiled these stories in his magnum opus the *Katha Sarit Sagara*, written in the 11th century. The second major work belongs to Shivadas prepared in around the 15th century.

The narrative involves the story of king Trivikramasena, or the legendary Vikramaditya which can be read both on literal and metaphorical planes. The story narrates that king Vikramaditya, was mysteriously visited by a *tantric yogi* named Kshantisheel on regular intervals. Kshantisheel gives him a fruit as a gift and disappears without saying a word. The king later discovers that the fruits contain precious gems concealed in them.

The king is profusely indebted to have received rare and precious gifts from the *yogi*. Being extremely righteous, the king is under obligation to return the favour and asks the *yogi* what he wants, in return. The *yogi* asks him to help him in his spiritual occult pursuit, by bringing *Vetaal*, a dead body possessed by a spirit, for a ritual which he is performing. It is a herculean task, which could only be performed by someone supremely righteous and brave, for it was no cake walk to capture *Vetaal*, the dangling upside down on a sesame tree, in a dark and spooky cemetery. No doubt the narrative runs like a mysterious gothic saga with embedded hyperlinks to undecipherable mystic and spiritual codes.

As the narrative proceeds, it becomes evident that capturing the elusive *Vetaal* is a penultimate challenge even for the valiant and righteous Vikramaditya. *Vetaal* sets the narrative into a supernatural setting of a land beyond death and an individual's struggle of return. *Vetaal* agrees to go with him only on his own strange terms and conditions, as if specifying the rules of the deadland: *Vetaal* directs that he would go with the king only if he didn't speak and utter a word on the journey.

The complexity of the narrative is enriched by yet another device: a paradoxical riddled narrative structure. During the course of the journey, *Vetaal*, tells a story that ends with a riddle. If the King cannot answer the riddle correctly, *Vetaal* agrees to remain in captive. *Vetaal* drafted the conditions quiet thoroughly. If the king knew the answer but still kept quiet (which was anyway less likely due to his righteous qualities) then his head would burst into a thousand pieces!

The terms come with a catch as Vikramaditya, the king with flawless sense of judgement was expected to know the answers to the riddles, which in turn meant that his solving the riddle would release *Vetaal* and render his mission futile.

However, there was hope of salvation. If the king dint know the answer to the riddle, then he could remain silent and carry *Vetaal* back! So, the victory lay not in knowing, but in not-knowing!

As the narrative proceeds the king answers the riddles correctly and with each correct answer the *Vetaal* escapes and returns to the tree. Thus, though warned to remain silent the righteous king, paradoxically speaks to solve the riddle and consequently the cycle of catching and releasing *Vetaal* continues twenty-four times.

On the twenty-fifth attempt, the *Vetaal* narrates the story of a king and his son who are lost in a forest and pulled away from their army after their victory in a devastating war. They find the queen and the princess of the defeated enemy apparently alive and observe their footwear from which they can make out that the women have beautiful feet.

The king decides to marry the lady with bigger feet and says that his son should marry the girl with small, beautiful feet. It so turns out that the princess' feet were larger than her mother's! However, being true to their words, they abide by the code of rightful conduct which required them to keep their promises and act their speech. In due time, the son marries the queen and the father marries the princess. Eventually, the son and the queen have a son, and the father and the princess have a daughter.

After narrating this story *Vetaal* asks the king, as to what it was relation between the two new-born children? The question stumps the king as the complex relation was beyond the realm of valid, legitimatisation. Finally, *Vetaal* agrees and allows himself to be taken to Kshantisheel.

On their way, *Vetaal* shares yet another story, but this time it is in a flashback mode, without the typical riddles, which by this point in the narrative are almost synonymous with him. He confides that his parents did not have a son and that Kshantisheel blessed them with twin sons on a condition that both be educated under him.

Vetaal was taught much more than his brother but was often ill-treated, whereas his brother was hardly taught much, but was adored. *Vetaal* became miserable until he came to know reason behind Kshantisheel's behaviour. Kshantisheel had planned to give his brother back to his parents and had planned to sacrifice *Vetaal* whom he had purposefully groomed as an '*all-knowing kumara*'.

The paradox of 'knowing' verses 'not-knowing' is a theme which runs throughout the text. Vikramaditya could not release the elusive *Vetaal* as he knew the answer to all the riddles. Likewise, *Vetaal* was to be sacrificed as he was an 'all-knowing' *kumara*, or a young boy. The theme of knowledge and suffering is closely linked in several spiritual texts; the close imagery of the birth of suffering after Eve eats from the 'tree of knowledge' on being tempted by the serpent is a popular percept. Yet, knowledge and awareness are paradoxical to evolution and development. Unless we become aware and increasingly so, we don't develop and if we do develop, development has a cost. The theme of 'not-knowing' and 'knowing' in the narrative appear like twin situations, which are paradoxically interrelated and need to be carefully balanced by skilful spiritual adepts on their journey to spiritual evolution.

The narrative proceeds and *Vetaal* discloses that by sacrificing him Kshantisheel could become immortal and rule the world using his *tantric* or occult powers. He also reveals that now the Kshantisheel plans to sacrifice the king too. He reveals that Kshantisheel would ask Vikramaditya to bow before his patron goddess Kali and would behead him as he bowed. He would then take control over the *Vetaal* and sacrifice his soul.

Vetaal suggests that the king should ask Kshantisheel, how to perform his obeisance, and then behead the him while he demonstrates the ritual. The king follows *Vetaal* and after he beheads Kshantisheel, he is blessed by Lord Indra and Devi Kali. *Vetaal* who is finally free offers the king a boon, and the king magnanimous king requests that Kshantisheel's heart and mind be cleaned of all sins and his life be restored as a good living being. *Vetaal* is pleased by his act and promises that he would come to the king's aid whenever needed.

The narrative ends on a happy note and seems like a myth meant for child-like fantasy fiction. However, critical reading of the narrative can reveal information of a more profound nature.

An archetypal reading of the narrative, on a fundamental level, reveals three significant points, in terms of—(a) a standard sequence of events; (b) a general sense of meaningfulness and completion, in contrast to the post-modern existential meaninglessness in literature; and (c) a pervading sense of morality and a belief in the victory of "Good over Evil".

The narrative of *Vetaal Panchavimshati* is replete with archetypal images and symbols such as the Hunter, the Enchanted Forest, the Lady of the Lake, the King, the Prince, the Minister's Son, the Lake, the Pond and the Old Woman. The tales also contain symbolic gestures which can connote different meanings. It is a fact that in the field of performing arts, Indian classical dance tradition uses different gestures to communicate and narrate a story.

All the twenty-five stories are set in specific locations, some of which like Ujjain and Banaras are still in existence and thus provide historic credibility to the tales, even though they content remains more mythic than historic. While the location has been specified in each of the stories, the setting in terms of time, has either not been narrated, or has been lost through its transmission through the ages. The names of several locations such as Avanti and Shobhavati and characters such as king Yashodharman and Madansundari are repeated in the story.

The typical pattern of the plot where the Hunter King, over-whips his horses, who go astray and lead him into wilderness of the forest, where he loses his heart to a beautiful maiden; is reiterated in several stories. The theme of the story draws close parallels to the pool of myths in India and across cultures.

The stories twist the plot towards a complicated riddle. The narrative continues till the riddles can be resolved within the bounds of *dharma* and righteousness and justice prevails. However, the twenty-fourth riddle, pertains to a problem, outside the purview of natural sense of justice and is left unresolved by the king known for his great sense of Justice. With the riddle unsolved, the chain is broken and the narrative ends. As long as king Vikram can unknot the knot, the story continues, but with the knot untied, the narrative comes to a final full stop.

The narrative which appears simple and mystic can be interpreted as a didactic allegory like the later variants—*Gulliver's Travels* or *Animal Farm*. It can also be interpreted as a fictionised version of a real-life king, Vikramaditya, whose biography was transmitted in literature through accounts which eventually turned into myths, seemingly for a didactic purpose.

The truth remains concealed and cannot be known. However, what we have available is a tale which can be read metaphorically rather than literally as the message and content of the original source has been modified through the successive ages of a gigantic transmission. The factual account and epigraphic evidence in support of the hero is nearly non-existent. Despite the large number of accounts which eulogise him, what we have is an assortment of distorted myths.

Among the popular myths which thrive still in popular Indian culture, is *Vetaal Panchavimshati*, whose actual source being written in the extinct language Pishachi, can never be established. Thus, what we have is in Eliot's words, is a 'heap of broken images'.

However, whatever little is left which us has a residual value in terms of three peculiar features: (a) archetypal symbolic content, (b) archetypal universality emotion of appeal, and (c) archetypal continuity of existence beyond successive generations in time. Thus, we infer that if we are to draw from the story, we can with certainly outline the qualities of the king as they are universal and eternal. Therefore, we remember king Vikramaditya as a paragon to virtues, as a highest benchmark of standards which the Indian kings since eternity have tried to emulate.

However, the narratives such as *Vetaal Panchavimshati* include archetypal information which can provide information, in addition to the qualities of the legendary king Vikramaditya. Thus, fragmentary narratives of the dark chambers of history have scattered broken snippets of meaning which we need to puzzle out to fit into a most plausible picture.

East-face representing Childhood

North-face representing Old age

South-face representing Youth

West-face representing Maturity

Picture 7: Pashupatinath Temple, Mandsaur, Ujjain

4.2 The Monomyth of Vikramaditya

The dawn of post-modernism witnessed a man, Joseph Campbell who passionately devoted himself to the study of world's mythic traditions and spoke about the 'Monomyth', which he called, "Mankind's one great Story." He put forth that the myths of different cultures throughout the world, share a common structure which he broadly classified as: separation, initiation, and return. He proclaimed the archetypal Hero as a spiritual seeker, hidden within us, typical stages of whose life, mirrored the myths.

The myth of Vikramaditya as the saga of an archetypal the Hero, typically confirms to the archetypal structure of the 'monomyth' and is analogous to the mythic parallels of several cultures. This section undertakes to examine the narrative of *Vetaal Panchavimshati* with respect to the elements of the Monomyth. The narrative of *Vetaal Panchavimshati* discussed in the previous section has been drawn from the Sanskrit retellings of the mysterious *Brihat Katha*, originally authored by Gunadhya, in the esoteric language Paishachi.

4.2.1 Monomyth: A Hero's Journey

Campbell described the monomyth as a common pattern of narrative structure appearing in myths, epics, dramas, and other forms of narratives, right from the beginning of storytelling, down to our present age. It narrates the typical adventure of the archetypal Hero, who goes out and achieves great deeds on behalf of a group, tribe, or civilization. His journey, often more spiritual than literal, is marked by typical stages of trials, which are a common substance of all myths.

4.2.2 The Ordinary World

The Hero is introduced to the readers in the context of a paradox, problem or dilemma which eventually awaits him. He is juxtaposed against a background of environment and factors such as heredity and personal history. For instance, in the myth of Shree Krishna, the narrative opens with the description of atrocities inflicted upon vulnerable people including his own sister Devki, who would eventually give birth to Shree

Krishna, the redeemer born to protect people from Kansa. The narrative describes him as a child-hero, to describe his ability and preparedness, to face the trial which awaits him.

The narrative of *Vetaal Panchavimshati* introduces reader king Vikramaditya, and emphasises the exemplary virtues he possesses such as his extraordinary sense of justice, valour, and righteousness. The narrative also describes mysterious Kshantisheel who practises occult and foreshadows the trials to come. The opening of the myth, hints that the Hero is likely to face a tough challenge or an ordeal in near future.

4.2.3 The Call to Adventure

The Hero is called to adventure, either from situations taking place externally or from profound internal urge rising from deep within, irrespective of the source, the Hero must face the trial. In the epic Ramayana, Lord Ram is recalled to adventure after his marriage, just as he is set for coronation as the king. The old hunchback maid Manthara hatches the plot and convinces the young Queen Kaikeyi to insist that her son Bharat be crowned as the king. However, it is apparent that destiny herself reveals the trial before the young prince Rama, who after a series of trials matures as a the most exemplary king. Lord Rama accepts the call with the code of conduct fit for a warrior.

Sometimes, the archetypal hero contemplates and considers refusing the call to adventure. However, he has little choice but to finally accept the call and sets on to embark the journey. The Hero feels the fear of the unknown and tries to turn away from the adventure, but ultimately resolves to undertake the journey.

In the narrative of *Vetaal Panchavimshati*, the tantric Kshantisheel persuades the king to bring *Vetaal* hanging from the sesame tree in the cremation ground for the occult ritual he is performing. The archetypal hero is aware of about dangers not being able to accomplish the mission or the aspect of not being able to return. The King Vikramaditya is indebted to the tantric due to the gifts he bestowed him and being righteous decides to help him. The refusal to call is not explicitly stated in the narrative and king Vikramaditya seems focused and determined to accomplish the task. The qualities of his signified most certainly valour and strength of the mind and will become apparent through the narrative.

The call to adventure is similar to a call for self-improvement on a spiritual path. The spiritual aspirant has to face the dark, limiting forces of his own personality to become a Hero, a ruler of his own mind and body.

Swami Niranjanananda Saraswat, the Paramacharya of Bihar School of Yoga, Munger, in his book *Mind, Mind Management and Raja Yoga*, says:

> Raja means king and the name was given as an indication that with these practises one will become the ruler of one's own life, one's own mind. Thus, raja yoga consists of practises which allow you to become the ruler, the king of one's own life. You have to understand the intent of becoming a ruler. A king has many responsibilities. He has to look after many areas. He must possess the overall picture of everything that is happening in the kingdom. A king is not the manager of a department but has to control many departments together. Similarly, when you embark upon the journey of raja yoga, you have to be attentive to many things, as the mind is a subtle *indriya*, sense organ. (110)

4.2.4 Meeting with the Mentor

The Hero encounters a seasoned traveller of the worlds who gives him or her training, equipment, or advice that will help on the journey; or he internally reaches within, a source of courage and wisdom. In the epic Ramayana, Lord Rama meets god Hanuman who aids him in his journey of finding his wife goddess Sita and in defeating Ravana. In the epic Mahabharata, Shri Krishna comes to the aid of the Pandavas and their wife Draupadi, during all situations of hardship and provides them the right direction as the most capable and Supreme Guide. The place of a *guru* in Indian philosophy is compared to parents because the parents grant life to their children and the guru facilitates the process of a disciple's 'rebirth' as better and more capable individual. The popular Sanskrit shloka which reverberates in Indian culture, puts forth the significance of a guru:

> *Gururbrahma gururvishnu gururdevomaheshwarah I*
>
> *Guruhsakshashat parabrahma tasamai shrigurave namah II*
>
> [Realise that the Guru is Brahma Himself. He is Vishnu and He is also Shiva (Maheshwar). Guru is Parabrahma (Absolute Truth). With this knowledge I offer my obeisance to the Guru.]

The king meets *Vetaal* who will prove to be his most trusted mentor. *Vetaal* gives him advise in the form of a challenge—each time the king tries to capture the *Vetaal,* he would tell a story that ends with a riddle. If the king cannot answer the question correctly, *Vetaal* would consent to remaining in captivity. If the king knows the answer but still keeps quiet, then his head shall burst into thousand pieces. And if he answers the question correctly, *Vetaal* would escape and return to the tree. The *Vetaal* goes on quizzing the king till he finally gives up and acknowledges that he doesn't know the answer. The self-identity of the king as an 'all knowing' adept is broken and consequently a new, spiritually more advanced sense of self is created.

4.2.5 Crossing the Threshold

The archetypal Hero leaves the threshold ordinary world and routine-life and enters a new plane of somewhat supernatural existence, over-cast with unfamiliar rules and values. The Heroes in myths often enter enchanted forests, where the laws of ordinary land do not operate. Shakespeare made use of this convention in his popular plays *A Midsummer Night's Dream, Twelfth Night*, and in *As You Like It.*

The enchanted forest appears as a supernatural realm in the plays which acts as a natural catalyst that bring about a moral reformation of the characters and is a setting which resolves the conflict in the play. Illyria in *Twelfth Night* and the forest of Arden in *As You Like It* are such enchanted places. In *A Midsummer Night's Dream* also, the forest is a haunt of the fairies is a space where the natural and the supernatural intermingle and realistic and fantastic elements blend.

In the narrative of *Vetaal Panchavimshati*, the king agrees to *Vetaal's* unfamiliar rules and conditions and decides to undertake the journey in the dark, dangerous, unknown realm. The journey into the dark also represents the movement of the mind into the perplexing and confusing labyrinths of the unconscious self, which is the storehouse of content repressed memories, unfulfilled desires, undecipherable images. The foray into these labyrinths of the mind can be risky as people can get stuck and become depressive, irritational, and perplexed. Only those skilful adepts who possess valour or rather the strength of the mind and will can come back after resolving the mental complexes. With the complexes buried deep in the unconscious, they can become more matured and balanced beings and emerge as *raja yogis*—the rulers of their own mind.

Ujjain, the capital of Vikramaditya is a spiritual city which has been the sacred station of many spiritual practises including *Raja Yoga*. The presiding deity of the city Lord Mahakala himself is worshiped as *Maharaja*, or the divine king, the supreme *yogi* and founder of Yoga. The Shavite tradition is known to have existed in Ujjain, as evident from epigraphic and numismatic evidence, during the 1st century BCE, and through the proposed period of reign of the monarch and the tradition continues till the present time. The influence of the Yogic traditions, marked by different stages of spiritual development of a yogic practitioner, on the narrative of *Vetaal Panchavimshati*, therefore is highly probable.

4.2.6 Tests, Allies, and Enemies

The Hero faces trials and challenges in the dark plane, beyond the bounds of the familiar threshold of conscious awareness. As he journeys into the unknown territory where the laws of established governance do not hold any relevance, he travels enchanted, much as we do in dreams. He comes face to face with his enemies which may appear in myths as ogres, giants, and demons who he defeats with his good faculties. The story of the archetypal hero resonates with the shared story of mankind, where the Hero journeys into the uncharted territory of the unconscious to remove the root of evil, which becomes an unconscious influence of his behaviour.

In the epic Ramayana, Lord Ram travels through different location in search of his wife, who has been abducted by Ravana or Dashanan, the evil king of Lanka with his ten heads (*dash* means the numeral ten in Sanskrit) each of which represent ten vices: *Kama* (lust), *Krodh* (anger), *Moha* (delusion), *Maatsyasya* (envy), *Lobha* (greed), *Mada* (pride, stubborn-mindedness), *Buddhi* (can be closely translated as intellect or rather the tendency of the *Buddhi* to connect with sense objects which in turn give birth to desire, the root of suffering), *Manas* (can be closely translated as mind or rather the turbulence of the mind), *Chitta* (can be closely translated as the unconscious which contains the repressed memories, archetypes, and *samskars*, etc.) and *Ahamkaar* (*Aham* is a word for the self in Sanskrit and *Ahamkaar* can be most closely translated as the ego, or the sense of self-identity).

The encounters of Lord Ram, after he decides to travel to Lanka are also narrated in the epic, to name a few; he meets Sugreev and helps him in defeating his evil brother Bali. He also builds a bridge and crosses the sea which separates Lanka.

In the narrative of *Vetaal Panchavimshati*, Vikramaditya undergoes a series of trials in the form of riddles. It is evident that he clears the trials through his mental faculty of sound judgement and chases *Vetaal*, with a determined will and persistent effort. It is apparent that the king can face the challenge with a steady mind and is unperturbed by the paradox which could have kept him trapped in the strange land in a perpetual struggle to catch *Vetaal*. However, with a steady mind, strong will, good virtues and persistent effort, he is able to eventually transcend the paradoxical situation.

4.2.7 The Ordeal

Towards the middle of the story, the Hero enters a central space in the special world and confronts death or encounters his greatest fear. It is out the moment of death that he is renewed with a new life. In the epic Ramayana, when Lord Ram and his brother Lakshman fight with Ravana and his army, Lakshman is hit by an arrow shot by Ravana's son Meghnaad and falls unconscious. The bleak situation of the narrative is however overturned by Hanuman who flies and lifts the mountain Dronagiri and comes back with the mystic neuro-herb 'MurthaSanjeevior' popularly called Sanjeevi, which restores Lakshman to new life.

In the narrative of *Vetaal Panchavimshati*, after *Vetaal* agrees to go with the king, he reveals to him that Kshantisheel plans to sacrifice the king to goddesses Kali. The king visits the *tantric* Kshantisheel in the temple of goddess Kali and confronts death without fear. As *Vetaal* had revealed the plot and suggested that he kill Kshantisheel instead, the king follows.

The journey of the archetypal hero bears resemblance with the stages of a learner of the yogic practise. To quote Swami Niranjananand Saraswati, once again:

> The yogis say that the final hurdle to cross in the process of self-realisation is the ego. Therefore, in the final stage of spiritual life one needs the guidance and inspiration from a guru.... The guru channels the ego, changes its direction. This process is called egodectomy. Not all can go through egodectomy. Therefore, gurus don't have many disciples. They may have thousands of initiates but they have only one or two disciples on which egodectomy can be performed successfully.... The old self has to die. The shell has to be broken for the seed to sprout. As long as the shell remains, the seed will never sprout. The shell has to be broken and that is egodectomy. (*Mind, Mind Management and Raja Yoga*, 25)

4.2.8 The Reward

The Hero takes possession of the treasure won by facing death. However, the story does not end here as the danger of losing the treasure again is eminent. In the epic Ramayana, Lord Ram is united with his wife after he kills Ravana. However, the narrative doesn't end here, the danger of their being separated again still lurks in the narrative.

In the narrative of *Vetaal Panchavimshati*, Vikramaditya kills the tantric and *Vetaal* tells him to ask for a boon. King

Vikramaditya asks *Vetaal* to forgive Kshatisheel for his sins and prays that he turns into a person with a cleaner, purer heart. Death in the narrative brings a new life and Kshantisheel, who wanted to be a powerful ruler, but with the wrong intentions of vested selfish interest rather than for the public welfare. His death comes with the restoration of life and with the promise his spiritual growth as a better person. Vetaal rewards the king by promising to come to his aid, whenever he needs him. The trials of king are however, not over yet.

4.2.9 The Road Back

The Hero is driven leaves the special world and returns home with the treasure he has won to by braving the trials of his dangerous the mission and by encountering death. In the epic Ramayana, Lord Rama returns home with his family, the Hindus still light lamps and celebrate the festival of Diwali, to commemorate the event. In the narrative of *Vetaal Panchvimshti*, the king successfully brings Vetaal from the dark world of the dead to the everyday world of consciousness. He faces a near death ordeal but escapes the tantric Kshantisheel and eventually kills and restores him as a better person. The king returns to his kingdom unharmed and accomplished.

4.2.10 The Resurrection

At the climax, the Hero is severely tested once more, on the threshold of home. He or she is purified by a last sacrifice, another moment of death and rebirth, but on a higher and more complete level. By the hero's action, the polarities that were in conflict at the beginning are finally resolved.

In the epic Ramayana, goddess Sita has to take the test of Fire. She confronts the burning fire, from which she emerges unharmed as she is a chaste woman. In the narrative of life of Jesus Christ, Jesus is restored to life after he faces the trial of execution and is nailed on the cross. The mythic bird Phoenix, a symbol of restoration and life is a constant reminder of the evolving cycle of life. The evolutionary mechanism of the journey of the human mind is spoken of in the *Dashavataar*, the series of incarnations of the protector god Vishnu.

King Vikramaditya is said to have sacrificed his head 11 times before goddess Kali and each time he sacrificed himself, the goddess restored him to life. After his sacrifice, the goddess was appeased and proclaimed King Vikramaditya as a *Chakravarti Samrath*, a king of the *vidyadhaars* or the mythic demi-gods, who are air-spirits and attendees of god Shiva. In Jainism, the *vidyadhaars* are adept human *yogis* who possess *vidya*, or 'knowledge'.

4.2.11 Return with the Elixir

The Hero returns home or may even continue with the journey. He now bears elixir and as a transformed being, now has the power to influence people and transform the world around him.

In the narrative of Ramayana, Lord Ram rules his kingdom and his subjects are perfectly happy and contended under his rule. In the narrative of *Vetaal Panchavimshati*, King Vikramaditya rules his subjects with a sense of utmost justice, fairness, and a sense of welfare. He frequently visits his subject and ensures that their problems are fairly redressed. He encourages the development and literature and arts which blooms and blossoms under his rule.

The structure of the Monomyth and is characterised by stages bears an uncanny resemblance with the stages of spiritual development of a *yogic* practitioner. The story of the journey of Man, the archetypal Hero, with different faces finds its way in myths and in spiritual practises such as Yoga. The course of the spiritual journey of Man is imprinted in his mind and finds its way in different words and ways.

However, as we move in time, we constantly move away from this sublime source. As Man becomes increasingly connected with materialism, his faculties of spiritual senses, so-to-say are increasingly sealed. In this context, the mythic story of King Vikramaditya becomes the guiding inspiration for the heroes, who embark on journeys.

Picture 8: God Vishnu takes Varah Avataar to save the Earth, 5th century, BCE Udaygiri Caves, Vidisha

4.3 Vikramaditya and Arthur's Perceval: Archetypal Journeys

The legendary narratives of Maharaja Vikramaditya and king Arthur' knight Perceval serve as specimens of the monomyth with shared narrative structures exemplifying the "mystical religious quest" of the eternal spiritual problem of Mankind.

The legends share several common thematic concerns and motifs typifying the framework with connecting story within the story narrative. The legends, as archetypes represent a quest for the Self which remains hidden by the unfathomable depths of the unconscious. The narratives are inherently concerned with the projection of the Self, the difficult to access, challenging inner center. The myths figuratively represent the dominant collective consciousness and the journey of the archetypal Hero who undergoes the process of individuation and integration of the Shadow with the Self.

The legends portray similar situations where the heroes struggle against the dark aspects of divinity so as to awaken to heightened states of spiritual consciousness. They typically journey into the dark woods, meandering through riddled narratives and grapple with the dark until they come to a realization of the 'Imago-Dei'.

To reiterate that the narrative of *Vetaal Panchavimshati* was drawn from the much older narratives of the mysterious *Brihat Katha*, written by Gunadhya, in the esoteric language Paishachi. Pandit Somadeva compiled these stories in his famous work the *Katha Sarit Sagara* written in the 11th century. This section compares the narrative of *Vetaal Panchavimshati* with the legend of Perceval's quest, within the framework of the archetypal theory of literary criticism.

The legend of Perceval's quest appears in *King Arthur and his Knights of the Roundtable*, an Anglo-Saxon text from the 5th or the 6th century, which contains the account of Perceval's quest and encounter with the Holy Grail. Both the texts belong to the period of the Dark Ages share close structural similarities

The legends are similar on several counts. Firstly, they typify the 'problem of opposites' and the failure to recognize and integrate the shadow. King Vikramaditya undertakes to bring *Vetaal*, which can be interpreted in terms of the integration of the Shadow with the Self. King Arthur's trusted knight Perceval undertakes a similar mission in his quest for the Holy Grail.

Secondly, the Grail is a mysterious, "life-preserving and sustenance-dispensing vessel" which is guarded by a king in a castle, which is extremely difficult to find. The legend present the dilemma which foreshadows that the old and infirm king would certainly die, which will in turn make his land infertile unless Perceval, the archetypal Hero embarks on an impossible mission to search for the mysterious Grail. The narrative draws a close parallel with the story of *Vetaal Panchavimshati*, where the king embarks upon a dangerous journey to bring back the elusive and mysterious Vetaal.

Thirdly, in both the narratives the hero undergoes the challenge not due to a personal stake, but so as to help another rather commanding person. Perceval undertakes the journey to restore the old king, suffering from a mysterious wound due to which his kingdom is devastated. The king can only be restored to health if a—"knight of miraculous excellence finds the castle and, seeing what goes on there, asks a certain question". Likewise, the Kshantisheel, the *tantric* who instructs King Vikramaditya to undertake the journey needs *Vetaal* for a ritual which would bestow him unparalleled power, but only an "all-knowing *kumar*" could undertake such a mission, signifying a mentally strong adept prepared with emotional readiness to receive, a numinous experience of the inner center.

Fourthly, both king Vikramaditya and Perceval—epitomes of valour and righteousness set out on the difficult quest and fail several times, but remain fixed in their resolve, before they finally accomplish their mission. Perceval fails to ask the question, "about the origin of evil, the king's wound, and about the Grail's meaning" the first time he encounters the Grail Castle and the Grail. However, he is offered another chance and goes on several misguided adventures, loses many battles, takes wrong turns in the woods, and does not ask the "premediated question." Maharaja Vikramaditya answers twenty-four questions and each time the Vetaal goes back to the crematorium from where he is to be retrieved back. The several turns offered in the quest seem to represent the re-incarnating power of the Self.

Fifthly, the Grail Castle and the crematorium, dark, uncanny spaces, where laws of the ordinary world don't operate, identify which 'special world' of the monomyth and closely resemble the unconscious. The view of the concealed Shadow is available only to the one who is worthy, adept, and prepared to face the challenge.

Sixthly, the goal of narrative is not mere discovery of the Grail or possession of *Vetaal* but is rather Death of the old King as well as the *tantric*. King Vikramaditya kills the tantric, as Vetaal divulges his mala fide intentions of offering them as a sacrifice to goddess Kali. Likewise, with the secret words spoken, Perceval's royal ancestry is revealed, and the Grail is placed in his care, the ailing king, and his kingdom are temporarily restored.

Seventhly, both the heroes do not bring back the assigned Shadow figure to the promised assigners. Perceval remained at the Grail Castle and did not choose to take the Grail back to Arthur's court. King Vikramaditya did not entrust Vetaal in the custody of the *tantric* and instead befriended him.

The narratives end on a different note. As a result of Perceval's failure to return, the Grail disappeared with his death and went back into concealment, which represents a partial realisation. However, king Vikramaditya befriends *Vetaal* and after being blessed by the goddess Kali completes the archetypal journey and is proclaimed as a *Chakravarti Samrath*.

The three key questions associated with Perceval, address eternal concerns of human spirituality. The question concerning the origin of evil signifies that idea that "virtue breeds pride which leads to evil". Arthur's knights led a life of "high virtue" which naturally led to pride, which is inevitably perverted into evil. Likewise, the questions—"To whom is the Grail brought?" and "Whom does the Grail serve?" seem to be the archetypal turning points of the narrative.

Perceval's second question, "Whom does the Grail serve?" resonates with the questions "Whom does the Self-serve?" Does the Self-serve ego? Or Does it serve God's creation selflessly? Does the Self undergo the numinous experience of individuation? Is the Self available to continue the incarnation of the divine in whatever form it happens to be evolving in the universe?

The riddled questions in the narratives involve internalisation and self-examination. They bear a close resemblance with archetypal the process of individuation: the quest of redeeming the "Spirit of God in matter, under the guidance of the Self, to discover the essence of form what that means". The quest narratives signify a stage of development of the human consciousness beyond the material and concrete towards a symbolic meaning—the ability to discriminate between the polarities of good and evil, to rediscover the soul of nature.

Chapter 5
Immortal Memories: Notes on a Hero

5.1 Numismatics of Vikramaditya and the Archetype

The remains of visual artefacts for historical reconstructing are an accepted practise. The art, beyond its evidence as a visual document of history, tradition, and culture is also a symbol of archetypal essence. The iconography, gestures, and postures, with reference to narratives of myth, religion, arts, and literature, serve as specimens of contemporary traditions and regional culture. The interpretation of art as a signifier of a profound reality, an archetypal inner meaning presents an alternative dimension to the discourse. The intrinsic attributes of metaphysical, ritualistic, and aesthetic dimensions comprise the archetypal historical portrait apart from the outer form and style.

Indologists and art historians have interpreted Indian art within the context of Indian philosophy, myth, and religion. The questions such as treatment of space and time, human anatomy, in terms of proportion, and the evaluation against the Western Renaissance and Classical Greco-Roman art have been explored by Indian art historians. Coomaraswamy examined traditional Indian architecture from the artistic, historical, as well as from the metaphysical dimensions. He described the creative process in Indian art as the visualization of form through a process of "meditative internalization of yoga and its consequent realization by the artist in accordance with aesthetic conventions".

The eternal myths, symbols, manifest in forms of art, as an embodiment of the spirit of eternal space and time reverberate in expressions of art. The empirical evidence inscriptions, philosophic, religious, and literary texts in addition to mythic narratives and legends define the regional realities of the visual art.

Decoding visual codes associated with the ancient iconography through organised text-image studies is increasingly accepted. The studies typically involving iconography and iconology have evolved symbolically through their exploration in terms of gestures, postures, body positions, and the use of weapons, etc. The problem of correlating text and narratives to their expression in art forms resolving inconsistencies and decoding complex imagery which exits as a sacred riddle.

The conception of the ancient Indian artists as craftsman—the village or the urban artisans who were members of professional guilds, in service of a king, chieftain, or religious institution provides an outward projection of the artist and defines his role in terms of the societal relations, position, and class.

The idea or the abstract of art emanates to the artist from within the vast expanse of the unconscious and is conditioned further by his consciousness and cultural constructs. The influence of the archetypes of the collective unconscious realm are projection thus in artwork after being filtered and modified through the medium of his individual self. The archetypes of art display the eternal essence of artistic expression, existing as an integral yet individual depiction.

The archetypal thought is in congruence with the theories of Indian aesthetics and the ideas such as the '*asmita samadhi*' or the exalted state of artistic excellence typified by merging of the mind with the object of meditation. The artist as a creator undergoes a process of creative self-discovery characterised by relative elimination of the ego and realisation of the artistic object. The conception of art as an archetypal rendition concerns three key ideas—

(i) identification of recurring symbols,

(ii) identification of analogical inter-linkages of symbols with parallel cultures, and

(iii) interpretation of symbols with probable meaning.

The symbolic vocabulary of the numismatic art bears a testimony to the Vikramaditya tradition. The Purana coins or the 'punch-marked' coins, which were in circulation in ancient India, bear archetypal evidence of the tradition of Vikramaditya. The hallmark of these coins is that they do not bear the name of any king and are rather characterised by a number of mythological symbols such as the sun (solar symbol), crescent moon (lunar symbol), animals (Pashupati tradition) such as the elephant, the cow, the horse, the bull, the jackal, and the lion or the tiger as well as archetypes of philosophy such as the *dharmachakra*, the chariot and the tree.

The symbols occurring on the punch-marked coins were derived from the nature, culture and most significantly from values and the belief system of the contemporary society. It is a commonly held belief that the primary value of coins was normally in a monetary sense but at the same time they convey a wealth of information which contributes to the historical and archetypal evidence. The interpretation of symbols appearing on the coins is shrouded with difficulties on account of the abstract and obscure nature of the evidence. In the opinion of Heinrich Zimmer:

> They are endowed with an almost incredible life-force; they outlive eras and the declines of civilizations. New generations are fascinated by them and they migrate to distant regions—from Mesopotamia, for example, to Cambodia. Ignoring silently the lapse of time, they can remain alive from the third millennium B.C. to the second millennium A.D. For they are like receptacles, ever ready to receive and to hold the essence of a new meaning. Differing generations and far separated cultures pour into them the contents of their hearts and imaginations. Whatever spiritual energies may be in need of adequate manifestations in the visible realm can find in them a tangible, meaningful

> pattern. They lend themselves willingly to the service of the most divergent functions, and so knit together, in a wondrous repetition, the whole adventure of man.

The symbols on the coins can be categorised into the broad archetypal categories of—'Universal' or 'Individual' and 'Chronological' or 'Time-bound'. The 'Universal' symbols are in congruence with the 'Chronological' symbols and are found as a recurrent motif on different epigraphic objects including coins. The archetypal themes manifest in consistently constant or modified forms throughout historical periods pertaining to different ages.

5.1.1 The Symbol of Ujjain

Picture 9: Symbol of Ujjain on punch-marked coin of 1st century BCE

The ancient art of any culture is, after all, the collective manifestation of the primitive spirituality. The symbols appearing in the Vikramaditya art are no exception and draw parallels with symbols of several cultures.

To discuss the first case, the symbol of Ujjain which typified by a cross with four circles at the end of each arm is closely associated with the tradition of Vikramaditya art as the legendary king is believed to have established his capital at Ujjain.

The symbol appears on coins of as early as the third century BCE belonging to the period of the Mauryan dynasty. However, this does not necessarily imply that the symbol did not exist earlier and is rather a part of a continuum of the great tradition which existed for a considerably significant prior period. The fact the symbol also appears on coins of other city-states such as Ahichhatra, Ayodhya, Eran, Iksvakus, Kannauj, Koshambi, Mathura, Rairh, Nagari, Rajgir, Uddehika, Yaudheyas and Satavahanas, indicates the 'Universal' attribute associated with the symbol.

Historians have expressed different readings of the symbol. Some of the interpretations based on probable evidence suggests that the symbol represents the junction of the four trade routes which intersected at Ujjayini, the contemporary Mahajanapada and a flourishing center of trade. The four circles have been interpreted as the four directions and the cross as signifying the intersection of the Tropic of Cancer with the Equator. However, it is clear that this idea is factually incorrect as though the Tropic of Cancer passes through Ujjain, it clearly does not intersect with the Equator. It follows that the symbol thus is suggestive of a meaning more metaphorical than factual.

The metaphorical connotations of the symbol have been examined by prominent historians. K.D. Bajpai and S.K. Chakravarti have interpreted the symbol as Vajra, the weapon of Indra, the king of devas. The Vajra draws associations with the iconic cross and ball motif, signifying the qualities of indestructibility and irresistible force.

Picture 10: Buddhist 'Vishva-Vajra'

The concept of Vajra is derived from the Sanskrit texts and connotes the dual properties of the thunderbolt and diamond, thus signifying vitality and strength. It was popularised as a spiritual symbol through Vajrayana, the tantric school of Mahayana Buddhism.

The double Vajra or the '*Vishva-Vajra*' constitutes four lotus mounted heads arising from a central node towards the four cardinal directions. It symbolizes the true nature of things, which is essentially, pure, and illuminating and at the same time, indestructible and indivisible. The symbol is representative of the indivisibility of wisdom and compassion and the union of male and female principles.

Another interpretation of the symbol of Ujjayini has been held by historians which hints at its association with the common Hindu symbol Swastika. A.M. Shastri indicates the connotations of the symbol with the Swastika, which is a popular solar symbol, characterised by the prototype of four cardinal directions and their intersection at the center. The depictions of sun and fire symbols are suggestive of a striking resemblance between parallel symbols of the world.

The archetypal symbols of the 'cross and the ball' have been used by different ancient cultures particularly during the Bronze Age. The French archaeologist Gabriel de Mortillet recognised them as not merely ornamental but rather as religious symbols of consecration used specially during burial ceremonies.

The cross a geometrical figure consisting of two bars that run perpendicular to each other appears in many cultures of the world and has become the icon of Christianity, symbolizing God's self-sacrificing love. The two intersecting lines drawn both vertically and horizontally are used as alphabetic symbols of several languages as well as in architecture, mathematics, art, religion, and culture.

The cross-shaped symbols and the Swastika have been used as sacred solar and fire symbols. Both Vajra and Swastika has also been associated with of lightning, thunder or tempest in the Aryan civilization. The Norse deity Thor and his thunderbolt can be regarded as a parallel to the Vajra. The Egyptian Ankh, the symbol of life, which closely resembles the cross is another illustration.

The figures bound by the cross are recurrent archetypes, whose code of spiritual geometry has been largely lost. The horizontal line in the cross conveys the idea of infinite time and indestructability while the vertical line represents indestructible force, which conveys the idea of the matter rising to meet the Spirit.

The symbol of Ujjain is a universal symbol of the truth of life. The symbol reverberates the essence of valour, indestructibility and irresistible force the epitome of qualities signified by the Vikramaditya tradition are eternally relevant across the world.

5.1.2 'Taurine Symbol' or the *Nandi Pada*

Picture 11: Taurine Symbol or the Nandi Pada on punch-marked coins of Ujjain

The taurine symbol or the *Nandi Pada* (Nandi's footprint) is a frequently occurring iconographic motif of the Vikramaditya tradition. The symbol resembles the Brahmi letter "ma" and the Devanagari numeral four and the English numeral eight. The symbol appears as a common motif in the punch-marked coins of Ujjain.

The symbol can be traced to as early as the Harappa Civilization and is closely associated with the Pashupath tradition of ancient Shaivism with numismatic data in support of the view of anthropomorphic representation of Shiva in the form of a bull. The symbolism of ancient Indian coins presents evidence of his depiction the theomorphic, anthropomorphic and phallic form. The close association between Nandi and Shiva further supports the view.

The famous 'Pashupati Seal' belonging to the Indus Valley Civilization depicts a seated figure, largely agreed to represent the primitive Shiva, who is surrounded by animals, one of which is a robust bull.

Picture 12: Pashupati Seal and the Taurine Symbol

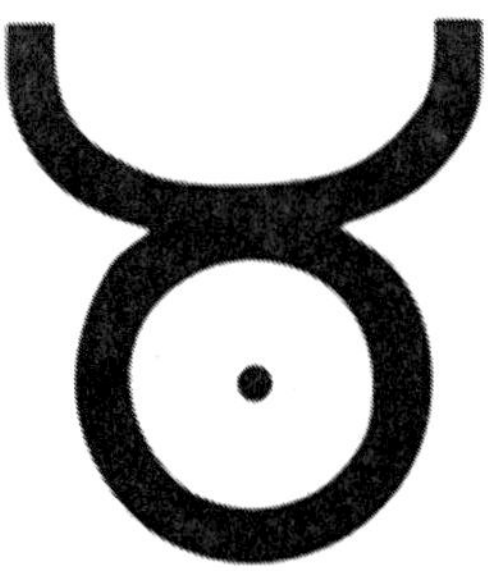

Picture 13: Taurine Symbol: Sun and the Crescent Moon

Picture 14: Taurine and the evolved Trishul

The symbol draws close association with Taurus an object associated with the cult of bull-worship since the Early Bronze age. It also represents the constellation Taurus the 'bull' which is located in the Northern celestial hemisphere. The association of the sacred bull as a symbol associated figures in different cultures.

In Greek mythology, Taurus is disguised Zeus in pursuit of his lover Europa, who was carried away by him while she gathered flowers on the seashore. The evidence of the cult of bull worship in ancient Egypt is evident from the sacred Apis, a holy bull associated with the worship of goddess Hathor for having known being ritualistically sacrificed and reborn.

Historians like C.S. Upasaka suggest the connotation of Mars or Mangala with the taurine symbol due to its resemblance with the first syllable of the Mangala spelt in Pali. The symbol thus is suggestive of the qualities of Mangal characterised by auspiciousness, good fortune, prosperity, and well-being. The view draws analogical parallels with the Druids who regarded the bull as a solar symbol associated with prosperity and wealth. The Chinese association of the bull as symbolic of a strong will and the Celtic connotations of symbolic of procreation reinforce a similar idea.

The bull as an archetype signifies the raw energy or the masculine brute force of life which man has tried to control since primitive times. The symbolism of bull is closely associated with the Shaivite tradition and the sacred bull 'Nandi' the mount and guard of the heavenly abode of Shiva is installed at the gates of all Shiva temples, facing the deity.

5.1.3 Six-Armed Symbol

Picture 15: Six-Armed symbol on punch-marked coins of Ujjain

The six-armed symbol is common symbol which appears on ancient Indian coins. It depicts a circle usually with a pellet in the center surrounded by six-arms/three-arrows heads/taurine symbols.

The symbols bear a close resemblance with the Buddhist symbol 'Paramitas' which is relevant particularly due to the prevalence of Buddhism in the Mauryan-age Ujjain.

The Buddhist concept of 'Paramita' is represented by a circle with six spokes and is associated with the idea of 'perfection'. The term is derived from the Sanskrit root '*Para*' which means the 'other shore' and metaphorically connotes the idea of going beyond our own notion of the self. It prescribes the performance of actions and attitudes are in a non-egocentric manner which and their internalisation through habit and practise. The spiritual progress of the soul through a non-egoistic orientation towards life and its manifestation in regular conduct of routine affairs is the underling belief of the concept.

Traleg Rinpoche in his work *Essence of Buddhism* explains the paramitas in the following words: "If we want to obtain enlightenment by becoming a Bodhisattva, it is necessary to actualize wisdom and compassion. This is done by the practice of what are called the six *paramitas*, or transcendental actions."

Picture 16: Dharmachakra and Paramitas

It follows that the paramitas represent six paramount mental states which are crucial for spiritual evolution in the journey towards attaining liberation and enlightenment including generosity, discipline, patience, diligence, meditative concentration, and wisdom. The spiritual states can be developed by a seeker through habitual cultivation and experience.

The hexagonal symmetry of six arms is a popular cultural motif and comes across as a symbol in different societies, religions, and cultural practices. The snowflakes with six symmetrical spokes are a symbol of Christianity and are used popularly as Christmas decorations throughout the world. They are associated with the symbolism of cloud as a messenger or a prophet. The snowflakes descend from heavens to the Earth and in the form of frozen water, an ancient symbol of truth.

Picture 17: Snowflake with Six Spokes

The Star of David, a star with six points, is a widely recognized symbol which appears on ancient artefacts of Judaism, consisting of two interlocking equilateral triangles. The arms of the star represent they foundational attributes of creation, which include *chesed* or kindness, *gevurah* or severity, *tiferet* or harmony, *netzach* or perseverance, *hod* or splendor, *malchut* or royalty and *yesod* as the foundation.

The six-armed figures can also be interpreted with reference to the six-armed manifestation of Mahakala, as a tradition of depiction in Shaivism, which has an ancient association Ujjain which continues till date with the city being celebrated as the hub of worship of the jyotirlinga of Mahakala.

The six-armed Mahakala, the consort of Mahakali, is the fierce and mighty emanation of the compassionate Avalokiteshvara in Buddhism. He is depicted as having six arms, which signify the successful completion of the six transcendental perfections: generosity, patience, morality, diligence, meditation and wisdom. Hinduism perceives him as the ultimate form of Shiva, the destroyer of all elements. He is perceived as 'maha' or great and 'kaal' or time as nothing exists beyond him—no element, no dimensions, and not even time.

Picture 18: Six-armed Mahakala

5.1.4 Three-Arched Hill

Picture 19: Three-arched Hill and Six-armed Symbol

The symbol of a three-arched hill symbol is a common motif engraved on the coins of Ujjain. The symbol is found on ancient coins belonging to different states and periods throughout India, though there are some variations to the number of the hills depicted, or in the symbol surmounting the hill, in the form of a crescent or a star.

The symbol is also associated with Buddhist symbolism and was popularised during the Mauryan age. It appears in coins of Malwa region along with the taurine symbol or the tree-in-railing symbol, the elephant, or the six arms symbol or the river or sun.

It has been argued to represent the imperial symbol of the Mauryas, though is not limited to it. The symbol has been agreed as a representation of the Buddhist concept of Chaitya or the Meru. The concept of Meru and Buddhist Paramitas are internally interlinked as they represent the spiritual journey of a seeker along a raised plane of consciousness exhibited by the Meru or a spiritual mount. The symbol of six mountains with a star on top is a popular motif in Christian symbolism which is a close parallel to the three-arched hill symbols.

Picture 20: Mountains and the Star

5.1.5 River and Tree in Railing

Picture 21: River and tree in Railing, Ujjain

The river and tree as symbols of Nature reinforce the ancient belief in the latent healing power of plants and water. The Vedic literature is suggestive of the view that plants were the first to emerge from the primordial water, the ultimate source of life. Several textual instances of the Vedas assert that *rasa*, the creative constituent of primordial water poured through the plants as sap and eventually the other forms of life including animals and humans evolved from plants. The *rasa* often metaphorically acknowledged as *soma* or *amrit* or the elixir of life flows through every living organism in the form of liquids such as blood or semen, the loss of which implies death and loss of fertility. The reverence to waters and the plants is evident in several Vedic hymns, invoked to bestow fertility. This idea reverberates in the lines, "Let the heavenly waters, rich in milk flow propitious upon thee; propitious to thee be the herbs."

The significance of water and plants is explicitly mentioned in the Hiranyakeshi Grihya Sutra, ritual of *annaprashan* or the occasion of feeding solid food to an infant for the first time, "I give thee to eat the essence of water and of the plants." The epic Mahabharata elaborates that the idea of churning of the Ocean and states that the *rasa* of plants on the Mount Mandara mingled with the water of the cosmic sea and transformed into milk, which created *amrit*, or the elixir of life.

The instances of river and tree-worship are evident since as early as the Vedic times. The personification of the auspicious qualities of the tree are interspersed in Vedic literature. The deification of plants as Mothers Goddesses, much older than the gods themselves, and their conception as powers who can heal, nourish, and strengthen life is an ancient belief which continues till date in the customs of Indian tribes. The tree is closely associated with the idea of enlightenment and wisdom and the representation as Buddha as a tree or being seated under the tree is a widely accepted symbol of Buddhism.

The punch marked coins of Ujjain bear the ancient symbol of the tree and the river at several instances. The symbol has been interpreted in the context of the Shaivite tradition prevalent in Ujjain. The tree is suggestive of the Vata Vriksha under which Shiva performed austerities and the river is probably Shipra. The tree often appears within a railing, as in case of the Buddhist art and the river at places consists of fishes.

Picture 22: Tree motif engraved on the main entrance of Sanchi Stupa

The sacred tree or the tree of life is an archetype which appears in several mythologies, philosophies, and religions of the world. The tree in its cosmic form is associated as a figure connecting the heaven with the underworld. In Norse mythology, for example, Yggdrasil is a mythical 'ash' tree that is the centre to the cosmos, and connects the nine worlds of Norse cosmology. It is believed to have nourished gods, humans, and animals, and served as a medium for their travel between the different realms. The Slavic tree of life stands upon rock Alatyr, from which all rivers originate.

5.1.6 Standing Shiva 'Mahakala'

Picture 23: Standing Shiva 'Mahakala', punch-marked Coin, Ujjain

The traces of Shaivite art have been found in Indian art since as early as the Indus Valley Civilization. The worship of Shiva as the benevolent lord Pasupati and the terrible Vedic Rudra has gone through phases of evolution into his reconciliation and transformation as Shiva. The depiction of Shiva on punch-marked coins in the three broad forms—symbolic, theomorphic, and anthropomorphic, has also evolved.

The depiction of Siva in human form is believed to have been represented for the first time on the coins of Ujjain and Malwa region. His depiction in human form with matted hair, holding a '*danda*' (staff) or a spear in his right hand and a '*kamandala*' (pot or pouch of water) in the left is a common motif of punch marked coins of Ujjain. The deity may have a reference to 'Mahakala' the presiding deity of Ujjain, of whom Maharaja Vikramaditya was an ardent devotee.

Picture 24: Deity with three heads

The depiction of a three-headed deity in few coins has remained a subject of scholarly deliberation. Cunningham interpreted the figure as 'Mahakala' a form of Shiva still worshipped in Ujjain. However, scholars such as Allan, identify him with the six-headed god Skand, with his three heads in front being displayed on coins and the three in the rear remaining invisible particularly due to the absence of the '*danda*' and '*kamandal*' or the trident or other symbols associated with depiction of Shiva on punch-marked coins.

The iconographic features of the male-female figures depicted on punch marked coins of Ujjain can be interpreted in the light of the Agama texts which outlined the 'Ardhnarishwara' form of Shiva. As per the concept of the depiction should be half-man and half-woman.

Picture 25: Male and female figures on punch-marked coins of Ujjain

5.2 Goddess Harsiddhi in the Vikramaditya Tradition: The Mother in Myth

The archetypal image of the Mother in myth is a metaphor of the collective expression of the unconscious. India has been the home of worship of *Prakriti* since the dawn of civilisation and the mythic narratives of the Mother in the Indian tradition are eternally relevant.

The reference to 'maternal archaic imago' in the myths of king Vikramaditya is distinctive. The narratives involve obedience the father figure of authority represented by the qualities of valour, justice, and reason yet at the same time, they proclaim the surrender of the self to the Mother as the fine feet of accomplishment.

The temple of Harsiddhi Devi in Ujjain is situated close to the memorial throne of king Vikramaditya on Vikram teela, where he is majestically seated accompanied by the thirty-two celestial nymphs. The goddess Harshidhhi is believed to have been worshiped and appeased by king Vikramaditya, through his righteous deeds. At his request Harshidhhi Mata, who was known by the name 'Mangalchandiki' in ancient ages, agreed to come to his kingdom at Ujjain, so that he could worship her regularly. The famous temple of Harshiddhi Mata is located at Ujjain still bears testimony to the myth.

The goddess Harshiddhi is considered to be a contracted form or at least, a form of "Harshad Amba", which means "The Happy Mother" and is regarded as one of the aspects of the goddesses Amba and Kali. The temple is among the most significant *shakti-peethas* or the devotional shrines where the severed body parts of the goddess Sati fell.

The myth behind the *shakti-peethas* is based on the story of the death of the goddess Sati, upon whose death, her consort god Shiva, carried her body, out of extreme grief reminiscing about their moments as a couple and roamed around the universe with it. In order to absolve the situation, Vishnu used his Sudarshana Chakra, to cut her body into 51 parts, which fell on Earth and become sacred sites which people visit to worship the goddess.

It is believed that king Vikramaditya dedicated his head eleven times in the feet of goddess Kali and the divine mother brought him to life each time. She was finally appeased and bestowed him the boon to become a "*Chakravarti Samrath*".

Pictures 26 and 27: Goddess Harshiddhi and Goddess Garh Kalika, Ujjain

Ujjain has been an ancient seat of Shaktism since ancient times and the worship of the goddess has the most significant place in the narrative of *Vetaal Panchavimshati*. In the myth, Kantisheel wanted to sacrifice the king in a temple of goddess Kali. Though in the story the king kills Kshantisheel, he later restores him as a person with a pure heart. Through the narratives of related myths it is revealed that Vikramaditya sacrificed his head eleven times before the goddess, who restored him each time to life and finally elevated him to the status of a supreme, all-powerful king. The authority of the goddess seems to have a place which is supreme in the narrative.

To sum up the contents and give a concluding word, this work sought to identify and explore manifestations of archetypes in mythic narratives on king Vikramaditya, through narrative analysis and critical reading. It attempted an archetypal portrait of king Vikramaditya based through the essays which provoked and archetypal rather than an empirical image of the king. The essays approach the old myths not with an orientation of a bygone past which would inevitably have little to offer and inspire; but with an approach that seeks to integrate the eternal relevance of myths, with the eternal journey of Mankind.

The essays with overlapping boundaries between the zones of myths, literature, and history, seek to augment the conventional narrative of Vikramaditya in which history and myths are attempted into segregated, rigid and mutually exclusive compartments.

Though the work in terms of structure and methodology, innovates the practise of an art, yet it takes care to renovate but not to mis-shape. Above everything else, the book seeks to preserve the glorious cultural legacy of the most iconic emblem of India and feels him as a constant presence, approachable in ourselves. The historic mystery of Vikramaditya can remain shrouded and sealed but the archetypal glimpse of the Hero, clearly reveals itself upon every discerning eye.

Picture 28: Vikramaditya Temple, Ujjain

Bibliography

"Ancient Coins, Satvahana Empire". Universal Numismatics. Aug. 2020. Web. 29 Aug. 2020. https://www.vcoins.com/en/stores/universal_numismatics/275/product/india_satavahana_empire_hilltree_type_lead_173_g_14x12_mm_obvthree_arched_hill_swasti ka_on_right__with_big_dot_below_partly_visible_ujjain_symbol_belowtree_in_railing/1268756/Default.aspx

Bajpai, K.D. *Numismatic Studies*, Vol. 2. New Delhi: 1992. Print.

Ben-Amos, Dan. "The Idea of Folklore". *Folklore: Critical Concepts in Literary and Cultural Studies*. Ed. Alan Dundes. London: Routledge, 2005.

Bhagwat, Durga. *The Indian Riddle*. Bombay: B.R. Bhatkal, 1965. Print.

Bodkin, Maud. *Archetypal Patterns in Poetry*. Oxford: Oxford University Press, 1978.

Burton, Richard F. Vikram and the Vampire. Classic Hindu Tales of Adventure, Magic and Romance. Project Guttenberg E Book # 2400. Release Date November 2000. Updated November 2016.

Campbell, Joseph. *The Hero with a Thousand Faces*. Third edition. Novato, California: New World Library, 2008. Print.

Chakrabarti, S.K. *JRASB, Numismatic Supplement*. No. XLVI, p. 63, 1936.

Chakravarti, M. *Malwa in Post Mauryan Period*. Calcutta: 1981. Print.

Clarke, R. *Northrop Frye "The Archetypes of Literature"*. 1951. Retrieved http://www.rlwclarke.net/Courses/LITS2307/2004

"Cross". *New World Encyclopaedia*. Web. July 27, 2020. https://www.newworldencyclopedia.org/entry/Cross

Daw, Muriel. "Paramitas (virtues) of Perfection: The 1987 Blavatsky Lecture at the Annual Convention of the Theosophical Society in England". *Blavatsky Trust*. Web. 29 Aug. 2020. http://www.blavatskytrust.org.uk/html/md_vos/vos_paramitas.html

Devare, Aparna. "Exploring Past Myths through Giambattista Vico and Jyotiba Phule". *Context to International*. Vol. 38(3), 2016. pp. 763-81. https://doi.org/10.1590/s0102-8529.2016380300002

"Dharam Chakra and the Paramitas" (Illustrated Image). Wikimedia Commons. https://commons.wikimedia.org/wiki/File:Chakra_Konark_Sun_Temple_N-OR-63.jpg

Dundes, Alan. *The Study of Folklore*. New Jersey: Prentice Hall Eaglewood Cliffs. 1965. Print.

Enlwistle, A.W. *An Introduction to Indian Histography.*1985. Retrieved Groniek Historisch Tijdschrift. University of Groningen Press. Accessed August 28, 2017.

Fraser, James George. *The Golden Bough*. Urbana, Illinois: Project Gutenberg, 2003. Retrieved http:// www.gutenberg.org/ebooks/3623 Accessed on June 21, 2016.

Freud, Sigmund. *The Interpretation of Dreams,* Third Edition. trans. A.A. Brill. New York: The Macmillan Company, 1913; Bartleby.com, 2010. Retrieved www.bartleby.com/285/ Accessed on July 24, 2017.

Frye, Northrop. *The Archetypes of Literature*. London, NY: Longman, 1951.

Frye, Northrop. *Myth and Metaphor: Selected Essays*. 1974-1988. Ed. Robert D. Denham, London: University of Virginia Press, 1990.

——. *Anatomy of Criticism: Four Essays*. Princeton, NJ: Princeton University Press, 1957. Citations are given parenthetically in the text as AC.

——. *Fables of Identity: Studies in Poetic Mythology*. New York: Harcourt Brace Jovanovich Publishers, 1984 (1951).

——. *Spiritus Mundi: Essays on Literature, Myth and Society*. Bloomington: Indiana University Press, 1976.

Greenblatt, S. 1999. *New Historicism: The Literary Criticism Web*. Retrieved http://www.ci.ber.edi/litcritweb.theory/newhistoricism.htm. Accessed on December 12, 2017.

Gupta, Arpita. "Ujjain Symbol". The Youngest Coin Collector. A blog dedicated to Indian Coinage. https://smallestcoincollector.blogspot.com/2018/01/ujjain-symbol.html

"Harshiddhi Temple". District Ujjain, Government of Madhya Pradesh. https://ujjain.nic.in/en/tourist-place/harshiddhi/

Harshiddhi Temple. Incredible India. https://www.incredibleindia.org/content/incredible-indiav2/en/destinations/ujjain/harshiddhi-temple.html

Hettiaratchi, D.P.E. The Symbols on the "Buddhist" Svastika coins of Ancient Lanka. ed. N.A. Jayawickrama. Paranavitana Felicitation Volume. Colombo: M.D. Gunasena & Co. Ltd. 1965. http://coins.lakdiva.org/ocr/dpeh_es.html http://fbcdnsphotosfa.akamaihd.net/hphotosakash3/734595_10200745791196574_112_n.jpg

Hutchenson, Linda. *Politics of Postmodernism*. New York: Routledge, 1989. Print.

Jain, K.C. and P.C. Jain. *Age of Vikramaditya*. Delhi: Agam Kala Prakashan, 2009. Print.

Jain, K.C. *Journal of Numismatic Society of Madhya Pradesh*. Vol. I, 1972. p. 15.

Jung, C.G. "A Psychological View of Conscience". trans. R.F.C. Hull. *The Collected Works of C.G. Jung: Civilization in Transition* (Vol. 10, 2nd ed.). Princeton, NJ: Princeton University Press. 1970 (original work published in 1958). Citations are given parenthetically in the text as PVC.

——. "A study in the process of individuation". *The Collected Works of C.G. Jung*. Vol. 9. Princeton: Princeton University Press, 1968.

——. "The Structure of the Unconscious". *The Collected Works of C.G. Jung*. Vol. 7. London: Routledge & Kegan Paul, 1916.

——. *Analytical Psychology: Its Theory and Practice*. New York, NY: Pantheon Books, 1968.

——. *Man and His Symbols*. New York: Laurel, 1977. Print.

——. *Memories, Dreams, Reflections*. New York: Pantheon, 1961. Print.

——. *Psychology and Alchemy*. trans. R.F.C. Hull. *The Collected Works of C.G. Jung*. Vol. 12. Princeton: Princeton University Press, 1968. Print.

Jung, C.G. and Beatrice M. Hinckle. *Psychology of the Unconscious: A Study of the Transformations and Symbolism of the Libido, a Contribution to the History of the Evolution of Thought*. London: Kegan Paul, Trench, Teubner, 1921. Retrieved https://archive.org/stream/psychologyofunco00junguoft/psychologyofunco00junguoft_djvu.txt Accessed on July 12, 2017.

Jung, C.G. and R.F.C. Hull. *Psychology and Religion: West and East*, 1969. Print.

Jung, C.G. "The Symbolic Life: Miscellaneous Writings". *The Collected Works of C.G. Jung*. Vol. 18. Princeton: Princeton University Press, 1968.

——. "A Psychological Approach to the Dogma of the Trinity". *Psychology and Religion: West and East*. trans. R.F.C. Hull. New York, US: Pantheon Books, 1969.

——. "Archetypes and the Collective Unconscious". *The Collected Works of C.G. Jung*. Vol. 9. ed. Read Herbert et al. trans. R.F.C. Hull. London: Routledge, 1991.

——. "The Spirit in Man, Art and Literature". trans R.F.C. Hull. *The Collected Works of C.G. Jung*. Vol. 15. Princeton, NJ: Princeton University Press, 1971. Citations are given parenthetically in the text as SMAL.

Jung, Emma and Marie-Luise Franz. *The Grail Legend*. New York: Published by Putnam for the C.G. Jung Foundation for Analytical Psychology, 1970. Print.

"Kali and Emperor Vikramaditya". Exotic India. Web. June 28, 2020. https://www.exoticindiaart.com/product/paintings/kali-and-emperor-vikramaditya-HD57/

Keith, A.B. *Indian Mythology*. Internet Archive Open Library Edition. US: Marshall Jones, 1917. Retrieved https://archive.org/details/indianmythology00carngoog/page/n6 Accessed on October 12, 2018.

Lanong, Rimika. A Study of Traditional and Modern Khasi Riddles. Diss. North-Eastern Hill University. 2012. Web. 30.3.2020.

Lord Raglan. *The Hero: A Study in Tradition, Myth and Drama*. London: Thinker's Library, 1949. Digital Library of India Item 2015.101509. Retrieved 25 August 2017.

Morgan, Clifford T., Richard A. King, John R. Weisz, and John Schopler. *Introduction to Psychology*. New York: McGraw-Hill, 1986.

Parks, George. "The Union of the Woman and the Man: A Jungian Model of Love Between the Sexes". ResearchGate. https://www.researchgate.net/publication/259289455_The_Union_of_the_Woman_an d_the_Man_A_Jungian_Model_of_Love_Between_the_Sexes

"Pashupati Seal" (Illustrated Image). Wikimedia Commons https://www.google.com/search?q=pashupati+seal+wikimedia+commons&rlz=1C1CHBD_enIN907IN907&source=lnms&tbm=isch&sa=X&ved=2ahUKEwit-KHovf_uAhVAzjgGHYGVAy4Q_AUoAXoECAQQAw&biw=1536&bih=666#imgrc=q2ugw4HrFzacdM

Petrov, Pier. "SS Goddess Civilizations and the Vinca script 5500 B.C. and the Black Sea Flood". Web. July 27, 2020. https://kachina2012.wordpress.com/2010/01/27/ssgoddess-civilizations-and-the-vinca-script-55oo-b-c/

Prince, Gerald. *A Dictionary of Narratology*. Lincoln: University of Nebraska Press, 1987.

Rajpurohit, Bhagwatilal. *Puranon Mein Vikramaditya*. ed. Shree Ram Tiwari. Maharaja Vikramaditya Shodhpeeth, Swaraj Sansthaan Sanchnalaya, Madhya Pradesh, 2012. Print.

——. *Sarvapracheen Vikramaditya Kathyein*. ed. Shree Ram Tiwari. Maharaja Vikramaditya Shodhpeeth, Swaraj Sansthaan Sanchnalaya, Madhya Pradesh, 2012. Print.

——. *Vetaal Panchavimshatika*. ed. Shree Ram Tiwari. Maharaja Vikramaditya Shodhpeeth, Swaraj Sansthaan Sanchnalaya, Madhya Pradesh, 2012. Print.

"Symbolism of Mahakala in the six-armed Manifestation". *Chinese Encyclopaedia*. Web. July 27, 2020. http://www.chinabuddhismencyclopedia.com/en/index.php/Symbolism_of_Mahakala_in_the_6-armed_Manifestation

Sang Kham. "The Six Protectors of Tibetan Buddhism". Web. July 27, 2020. https://www.tibettravel.org/tibetan-buddhism/six-protectors-of-tibetan-buddhism.html

Sarma, I.K. (1980). "Coinage of Satavahana Empire", Delhi, p. 69.

Saraswati, Swami Niranjanananda. *Mind, Mind Management and Raja Yoga*. Bihar: Yoga Publications Trust, Munger, 2013.

Sengupta, Sulagana. *Jung in India*. New Orleans, Louisiana: *Spring Journal*, 2013.

Shastri, A.M. "Religious Study of Symbols on Local Coins of Central India", No. II, p. 83.

Sircar, D.C. Ancient Malwa and the Vikramaditya Tradition. Ujjain: Scindia Oriental Institute, 1948. Print.

"Six Armed Mahakala. Eartly Eighteenth Century. (Illustrated Image). The Met. https://www.metmuseum.org/art/collection/search/37808

"Snowflakes" (Illustrated Image). Wikimedia Commons https://commons.wikimedia.org/wiki/File:Snowflake.svg "The Book of Abraham and the Facsimile Image-Part IV". NephiCode.com Web. 29 Aug. 2020. http://nephicode.blogspot.com/2013/02/the-book-of-abraham-and-facsimileimage_16.html

"The Six Paramitas: A Reader's Guide". Shambhala Publications. Web. July 27, 2020. https://www.shambhala.com/six-paramitas-readers-guide/

Tripathi, Radha Vallabh. ed. *Inventory of Sanskrit Scholars*. 2012. New Delhi: Rashtriya Sanskrit Sansthan, Deemed University.

"Ujjain, anonymous AE 3/8 Karshapana". Coin India Coin Galleries: Ujjain. Web. July 27, 2020. http://coinindia.com/ujjain272.jpg

"Vajrayana: The Diamond Vehicle". The Pluralism Project: Harvard University. Web. July 27, 2020. https://pluralism.org/vajrayana-the-diamond-vehicle

Vansina Jan M. Oral Tradition as History. University of Wisconsin Press, 1985. Project MUSE muse.jhu.edu/book/8436

"Visva Vajra" (Illustrated Image). Wikimedia Commons. https://commons.wikimedia.org/wiki/File:Faith_Buddhism_Vajra.svg#/media/File:Fai th_Buddhism_Vajra_BW_2.svg

Waddy Van. The Grail Legend by Emma Jung and Marie-Louise von Franz. March 9, 2014. Web. Accessed July 5, 2020. https://issuu.com/lewislafontaine/docs/grail

Wendy Donier. *The Hindus: An Alternative History*. NY: Penguin, 2009.

Weston, Jessie. *From Ritual to Romance*. Urbana, Illinois: Project Gutenberg. Release Date: May 2003. Retrieved 25 August 2017.

Wappen des Agostino Chigi (Illustrated Image). Wikimedia Commons. https://commons.wikimedia.org/wiki/File:Wappen_des_Agostino_Chigi.jpg Young-Eisendrath, Polly and Terence Dawson, eds. *The Cambridge Companion to Jung*. Cambridge: Cambridge University Press, 1997.